STRESS-FREE
NAVIGATION

Electronic and Traditional

STRESS-FREE NAVIGATION

Electronic and Traditional

DUNCAN WELLS

ADLARD COLES

LONDON • OXFORD • NEW YORK • NEW DELHI • SYDNEY

To the girls – Sally, Katie and Ellie

ADLARD COLES
Bloomsbury Publishing Plc
50 Bedford Square, London, WC1B 3DP

BLOOMSBURY, ADLARD COLES and the Adlard Coles logo
are trademarks of Bloomsbury Publishing Plc

First published in Great Britain 2019

A catalogue record for this book is available from the British Library

Library of Congress Cataloguing-in-Publication data has been applied for

ISBN: PB: 978-1-4729-6234-8; ePUB: 978-1-4729-6233-1;
ePDF: 978-1-4729-6235-5

4 6 8 10 9 7 5 3

Designed and typeset in 10.5 on 13pt Bliss Light by Susan McIntyre
Printed and bound in India by Replika Press Pvt. Ltd.

Bloomsbury Publishing Plc makes every effort to ensure that the
papers used in the manufacture of our books are natural, recyclable
products made from wood grown in well-managed forests. Our
manufacturing processes conform to the environmental regulations of
the country of origin.

To find out more about our authors and books visit
www.bloomsbury.com and sign up for our newsletters

All photographs were taken by or on behalf of Duncan Wells
unless otherwise specified

Synoptic chart on page 134 © British Crown Copyright 2013.
Used under licence from the Met Office.

Contents

Acknowledgements

Thank you to the Bloomsbury team – Janet Murphy, Penny Phillips – for commissioning this book and their excellent editing.

Thank you also to a team of people on whom I have leant heavily and who have all been keen to help:

Alan Watson (Raymarine)

Lance Godefroy (Navionics)

Lucy Wilson (Imray Charts & Imray Navigator)

Campbell Field of Field Yachting (Expedition)

Nigel de Q Colley (Expedition and B&G)

Daniel Conway (Furuno)

Bob Moshiri and the team (iNavX)

Phil Harris (Meridian Chartware)

AyeTides

Jelte (Savvy Navvy)

Tracey Cox, Dulcie Allen, Craig Davis and Rachel Oliver (Navico, Simrad, B&G, Lowrance)

Gavin Ashworth (PC Plotter)

David Ramos

Nadine Strathmann, Nadja Kneissler (Delius Klasing)

Mike Kerr (ChartCo)

Eddie Broadbent

Jonathan and Rebecca Parker

James Dillon

Don Cockrill MBE (UK, Maritime Pilots Association)

Dick Holness (East Coast Pilot)

Christopher Barker

John Cangardel (Canada)

Monique van Someren (Canada)

Bill Saint (USA)

Rob Bishop

Alex Whitworth (Australia)

Rod Snook

Jeremy Dale and Keith Friar (SeaSafe Systems) – for keeping me on the straight and narrow.

and Sally – as always.

▲ *The start of today's navigation: John Harrison's 'sea watch' (H4), completed in 1795 and accurate enough to allow us to measure longitude.*

Preface

This book came about because a student of mine said to me that occasional sailors wanted a book that would show them how to get a charter boat from the marina out to sea. A book that started on board with the electronic chart plotter.

And that is exactly what I show you in Chapter 2, 'On board'.

The simple fact about this clever technology is that the more we have, the more we need to know what it is doing and what it all means. For that we need to return to the basics – a paper chart, a magnetic compass, a plotter, a set of dividers and an almanac.

After all, if anything should happen to our electronic devices we will need to refer to our paper chart back-up.

But what our electronics can do for us is amazing. We can do it all manually, of course, but the electronics do the sums in a flash and they give us incredible detail and accuracy. Well, they will do if the data they are being fed is sound.

Don Cockrill MBE, Port of London pilot and one-time chairman of the UK Maritime Pilots' Association, told me: 'Today we know our position to within less than a metre on the Earth's surface. We are following the red course line on the digital chart. And yet we don't really know where we are. Not until we look out the window and we see the buoy that's marked on the screen in front of us. Then we know where we are.' And that is so true. The digital is fine, but we need to back it up with the fact.

Navigation is a fascinating subject and it is so broad, covering everything from oceanography to geometry, metereology, the universe, psychology, people management – the list is endless.

With this book you would easily be able to pass a Yachtmaster standard examination anywhere in the world. It is also for newcomers to sailing who may be setting out on a Day Skipper level course. Check what your course requires you to know and pick what you need from the book.

The key is the integration of the electronics, the chart plotters, radar and AIS and an explanation of what they are telling us.

Navigation is not a complicated subject, but it can be involved. I have done my best to distil the information and present it to the reader in a manner that allows for stress-free absorption.

I have tried to keep the thing as international as possible. Of course, many examples will come from home waters, the Solent for example, but we also look at East Coast America, Australia, the Baltic and France, to include our friends in other countries.

I will always start my passage planning by looking at a small-scale paper chart of the area I will be sailing but will then monitor my route on a chart plotter. Indeed, I will allow the chart plotter to take the lead role, but when offshore I will always plot my position every hour on a paper chart along with the log reading and the time. I will then fill out the log hourly with my speed over ground, course over ground, heading, wind direction, wind strength and pressure.

One other thing to mention about electronics and sailing a boat is that every member of crew needs to know how they work. I mean really know how they work. We have the ability to show different data on the screen – the chart, our position, heading, course over ground, overlaid with AIS (Automatic Identification System) or radar, wind data, lay line information, fish finder information, the seabed. To have the helmsman navigating in shallow water in fresh winds and calling for someone to set the repeater screen by the helm to show depth of water and no one being able to do this is a dangerous situation. The helmsman at this point is literally sailing blind. If I am sailing near the coast, whatever information I have on screen I will always include depth of water, or have an independent stand-alone echo sounder depth indicator.

And another thing: the motion of a boat tends to dull the senses, allowing us to become confused easily, so really knowing how to navigate round the screens of the chart plotter is essential for all on board.

Navigation at its essence is a matter of conning the boat safely and with due regard for your crew from one place to another.

There are videos throughout the book, which you can view by scanning the QR code on your smartphone. You can also watch these videos online at www.westviewsailing/stress-free-navigation-videos. For those following the RYA syllabus there are also the Westview Sailing tutorials videos, which can be accessed via www.westviewsailing.co.uk

◀ *Following the red line.*

▼ *The view out of the window.*

1 Introduction and philosophy

The fundamental difference between navigating on land and navigating at sea is that at sea you are navigating your way around a moving body of water. When you stop your car you can be reasonably sure that with the hand brake on, it will not move from this position. Not so with a boat. You may well have stopped the boat in the water, but it will be moving with the wind and the tide, over the ground, the seabed below. And this could be moving the boat into danger.

The other thing to consider is that on land the sea represents a danger. You can drown while swimming or get cut off by the tide. The sea can smash the shore and do damage. But when you are at sea you have to adjust your mindset. It is the land that is the danger. Hitting land when in a boat never ends well for the boat, or its crew. So when you are out there you want to steer well clear of land and ensure that at all times you have sufficient water underneath to be able to float.

Obviously you have to make port – and a copy of *Stress-free Sailing* or *Stress-free Motorboating* will make casting off and coming alongside a breeze – but if you can get into your mind that in a boat the sea is safe, the land is not, you will be well armed.

I am going to approach every element of navigation from the digital, first. I will look at the latest technology, designed to make our lives easier out there on the water. And then I will relate what's on screen to the analogue, the paper chart, so you understand what the screens are telling you.

Of course, there is always the possibility, however unlikely and however many electronic back-ups you may have, that everything will go dead. That is when you will need to fall back on your self-sufficient navigation skills. And these I will show you, so that you can find your position accurately enough and reasonably quickly, without any electronic aids.

In this book I have mentioned a number of chart plotters. This is not an exhaustive list as this is not

▶ *My trusty steed – Dorothy Lee.*

supposed to be a product review or comparison. I have just included examples where I have had access to the plotters. I am simply using this as an introduction to show you what the electronics can do and what it all means. And whatever products come along in the future, you will still need to know what they are telling you and what you need to do if for some reason they stop working all of a sudden.

Remember that putting to sea in any vessel, especially a small boat, is not without risk. I do not subscribe to the 'It's not my fault' culture that seems to pervade society these days, so let me make it quite clear that whether we are dealing with electronic or paper charts or pilot books, we do so at our own risk, we do so knowing that we need to cross reference information and that nothing will be 100% accurate or foolproof.

Don't follow any electronic aid blindly, look out of the window, look for the road signs.

You might wonder why astro navigation and the sextant are not mentioned in this book? Navigating by the stars is just the most wonderful, purest pure way to navigate and it is not hard despite the way some people present it. The satisfaction of fixing your position to within a couple of miles out on an ocean cannot be measured. But unfortunately there simply is not the space to include it here.

2 On board

You've just stepped on board. The kettle's on and tea will be along in a moment, so you switch on the chart plotter.

You will be faced with a warning.

Some say: 'All information is presented for reference only. You assume total responsibility and risk associated with using this device.'

Others may say: 'Not to be used for navigation', which I think is taking things a bit far, given that this is exactly what we will be using it for.

You then generally need to click the OK button to access the program.

I promised in the Preface that I would get you from your mooring out to sea the minute you stepped on the boat. You will have to get the boat from the dock to the fairway, but from here Navionics Dock to Dock, or Expedition or Adrena, or PC Plotter, or Savvy Navvy, or other apps that will no doubt come along, can do the rest.

From the home page, click on Chart and this is what you will see.

A chart with your boat – the blue triangle here – at the centre. You're not moving. You know that for a fact as you are tied to the dock.

The chart plotter confirms this by showing your Speed Over the Ground (SOG) as 0.0 knots. You can see the way the GPS thinks the boat is lying, which is your heading, from the aspect of the boat (the triangle) on the screen. It also gives you this as a compass heading at the top of the screen. It thinks your bow is pointing at 141° true.

The minute you start moving, your SOG will be displayed on screen, along with your Course Over the Ground (COG) and a line projecting forward from the bow of your boat. This line is your heading. 'Heading' shows the direction in which the boat

▲ *Chart plotter on.*

> ## LIMITATIONS ON USE
>
> This product is intended to serve only as an aid to navigation. Use of specific features such as AIS overlay, radar, and various cartographic aids are meant only to aid safety and decision-making. These features **cannot** be relied upon as complete or accurate as their use and availability may vary locally. It is **your** responsibility to use caution, sound judgment, official government charts, notices to mariners and proper navigational skill when using this or any other electronic navigational product.
>
> By pressing OK, I am stating that:
> 1: I have read and agree with the above disclaimer of liability, and understand the limits of proper use of this device.
> 2: This product contains embedded navigational charts provided by Navionics. By continuing past this screen, I agree to be bound by the terms of the Navionics End-User License Agreement, a copy of which is included in the documentation for this product.
>
> Press **OK** to continue

▲ *Warning.*

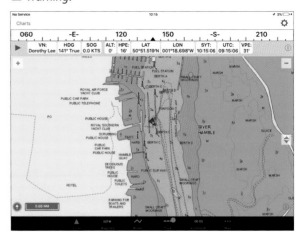

▲ *Tied to the dock, according to the plotter.*

is facing and is different from COG in that if you were going sideways your COG would show your sideways movement but your heading would show a line at right angles to this, indicating the direction in which your bow was pointing.

The latitude and longitude of your position is displayed at the top of the screen, along with your heading, the direction in which you are pointing and the time, which in the UK is UT.

Latitude and longitude are how we define our position on the surface of the Earth.

Let's go somewhere (the example shown uses Navionics Dock to Dock).

Follow the given route and you will get from the fairway out to sea in the English Channel by the Needles.

There, I have delivered on my promise.

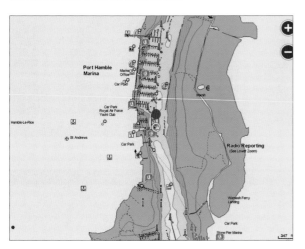

▲ 1. *Touch your boat on screen and a circle appears.*

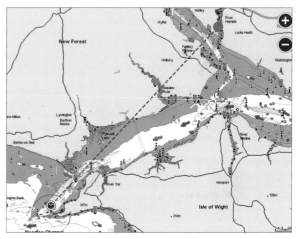

▲ 2. *Touch where you want to go to. Another circle appears and it draws a dotted line from here to your boat. Yikes! That's across land.*

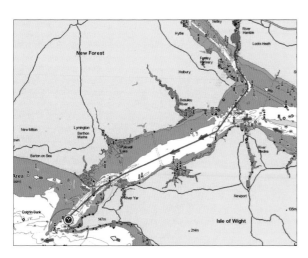

▲ 3. *It thinks about it for a moment and works out that you need a depth of water to float in and a safety margin, so it routes you down the river and to your desired location safely via the preferred channels.*

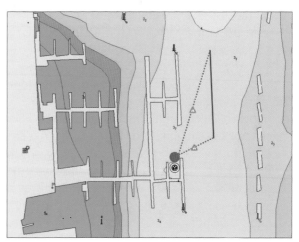

▲ 4. *Zoom in to see that you need to start from the fairway beside your berth.*

These programs will also warn you about dangers on the way.

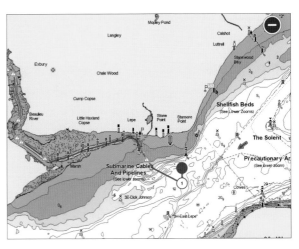

▲ 1. In the Solent, heading for Buckler's Hard up the Beaulieu River.

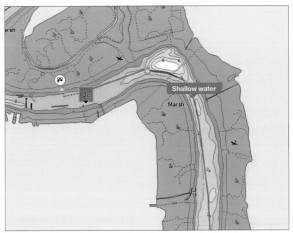

▲ 2. That's better – going by river rather than overland.

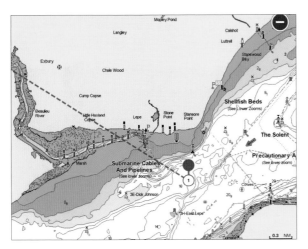

▲ 3. Dock to Dock warns us of dangers.

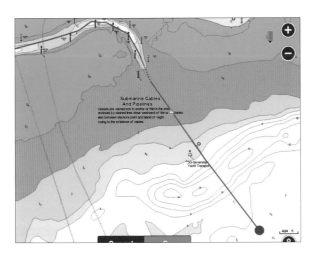

▲ 4. And it is not too keen on our destination. We will do our best not to run aground.

Once the program has given you the route, you should interrogate it and zoom in to see what dangers or obstacles you might meet. You then follow the route, looking out for the navigational marks on the way.

▶ *Here it has decided that my destination waypoint is too shallow.*

Parameters

The program is working to parameters that have been set either automatically or manually – the digital chart, a minimum depth requirement. It can access weather information, tidal height and tidal stream information and in some of the more sophisticated programs you can input optimum sailing angles for each sail and maximum wind speeds for the sails. Then when you set a route it will not only tell you which tack you will be on but also which sails you should set and fuel consumption if there is no wind. You can also limit the wave height you want to experience and the wind speed, in which case the program will tell you that setting off next Tuesday at three in the afternoon will be the ideal start time for the passage, as opposed to right now.

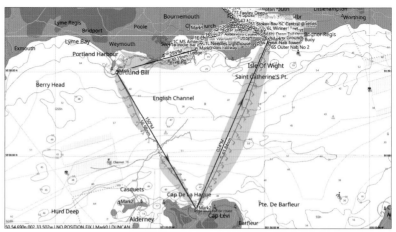

▲ *A passage from the Needles via Portland Bill to Cherbourg and the NAB tower, showing the direct route and then what we will actually be sailing according to the wind. The program has also allowed for the tide.*

▶ *And here is the detail, including which sail to use. Port tack is in red and starboard tack is in green.*

GMT Summer Time	Twd°M	Tws	Twa	Targ	Bsp	Set°M	Drift	Sail	Brg°M	Dist nm	Mo...	MSLP	Latitude
10-May-18 14:20	260	13.5	48	042	6.7	099	0.3	J2	209	1.85	Sail	1018.21	50 38.070
10-May-18 14:38	253	14.0	43	042	6.4	095	0.4	J2	207	1.77	Sail	1018.37	50 36.440
10-May-18 14:56	248	14.5	(33°)	042	6.3	087	0.5	J2	211	1.75	Sail	1018.52	50 34.852
10-May-18 15:17	245	14.8	(-20°)	042	6.4	082	0.7	J2	265	4.08	Sail	1018.67	50 33.337
10-May-18 16:13	238	15.5	(-40°)	041	6.4	072	0.9	J2	282	4.77	Sail	1018.92	50 32.908
10-May-18 17:04	233	15.9	-41	041	6.4	071	1.0	J2	278	3.57	Sail	1019.08	50 33.835
10-May-18 17:42	233	14.6	-46	042	6.6	078	0.8	J2	282	3.86	Sail	1019.22	50 34.274
10-May-18 18:20	235	13.6	-46	042	6.5	070	0.4	J2	282	4.11	Sail	1019.34	50 34.992
10-May-18 18:59	236	14.0	(-8°)	042	6.3	354	0.2	J2	246	2.70	Sail	1019.44	50 35.806
10-May-18 19:32	238	14.5	(38°)	042	6.3	264	0.5	J2	204	2.40	Sail	1019.55	50 34.658
10-May-18 19:55	238	14.8	42	042	6.4	241	0.5	J2	200	1.97	Sail	1019.67	50 32.457
10-May-18 20:13	239	14.8	(-19°)	042	6.4	230	0.5	J2	255	2.52	Sail	1019.75	50 30.593
10-May-18 20:39	240	15.6	97	160	8.0	231	1.4	J2	153	3.22	Sail	1019.81	50 29.901
10-May-18 21:03	243	14.3	97	160	7.9	246	0.9	A0	153	3.22	Sail	1019.92	50 27.055
10-May-18 21:28	242	12.3	93	161	7.5	259	0.5	A0	153	3.22	Sail	1019.90	50 24.217
10-May-18 21:55	240	11.1	88	042	7.2	262	0.8	A0	158	3.32	Sail	1019.87	50 21.387
10-May-18 22:25	237	10.0	86	042	7.0	266	1.2	J1	160	3.38	Sail	1019.80	50 18.327
10-May-18 22:56	229	8.9	85	044	6.8	264	1.3	J1	153	3.27	Sail	1019.72	50 15.181
10-May-18 23:29	219	7.9	77	045	6.3	266	1.3	J1	153	3.27	Sail	1019.62	50 12.288
11-May-18 00:04	200	7.4	64	045	5.8	247	1.5	J1	152	3.27	Sail	1019.52	50 09.412
11-May-18 00:44	180	6.5	76	044	5.3	246	1.4	J1	115	3.07	Sail	1019.38	50 06.554
11-May-18 01:30	162	6.3	(12°)	044	4.2	274	1.2	J1	169	4.05	Sail	1018.99	50 05.322
11-May-18 02:22	131	12.5	(-42°)	042	6.1	090	1.3	J2	159	3.53	Sail	1018.35	50 01.357
11-May-18 02:57	130	11.9	(-19°)	042	6.0	089	0.9	J2	139	3.05	Sail	1017.93	49 58.090

There are programs that work out the line you need to lay (lay line) to make the next mark. This is not just useful for racers, cruisers can use it too. For 'Lay line', the cruiser will be thinking 'Headland'. When do I need to tack to make the headland?

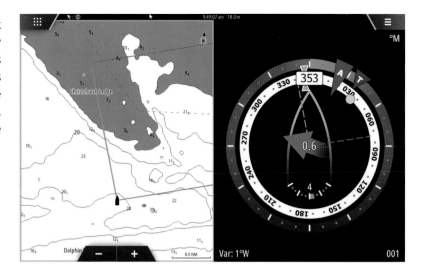

▶ *This is B&G's SailSteer program showing us when to tack to make the next mark.*

HOW THE CHART PLOTTER KNOWS WHERE IT IS

What is the chart plotter doing while it's warming up? Well, it is obviously not warming up. It doesn't need to warm up but it does need to think about things.

At the heart of a chart plotter is a Global Positioning System (GPS) and the first thing it needs to do is to find out where it is.

The many channels of the GPS receiver search the sky for satellite signals. Satellites transmit the exact time they send a signal. The GPS receiver knows the time the signal was received. By subtracting this from the time it was sent, the GPS receiver can tell how far away from the satellite it is. The GPS receiver also knows the exact position of each satellite in the sky when they sent their time signal and with the information from three satellites it can establish its position on Earth two-dimensionally. It requires a fourth satellite to get a 3D position, allowing for height.

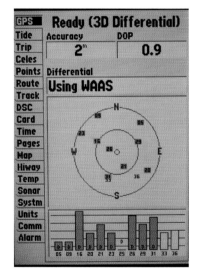

▲ *Green bars represent satellite signals received and strength.*

The system the GPS uses to find its position is known as trilateration.

Modern GPS receivers are able to receive signals from the two existing worldwide satellite systems, the American Navstar and the Russian GLONAS. The Chinese have a system called BEIDOU, which I am sure will be accessible once they provide global coverage, due by 2020. And of course Europe has Galileo which is expected to be fully operational by 2020.

A FEW QUICK TIPS ABOUT CHART PLOTTERS

1. Make sure you know how to unlock the touch screen.
Touch screen chart plotters will have a facility for locking the screen. This is because a chart plotter sited in the cockpit can start doing funny things in heavy rain. Manufacturers are working on developing screens that can tell the difference between fingers pressing on icons and rain hitting the screen, but currently there are occasions when you may need to lock the screen. So you need to know how to lock and unlock it. Each chart plotter will be different and you will need to look at the manual for your plotter.

2. Know how to centre the boat on the screen.
Occasionally you will scroll across the screen to investigate something, or you may have the screen set so that you follow your progress across the chart and leave the boat behind, so it is important to know how to centre the boat on the screen. Again, refer to the manual. Many chart plotters will have a button marked 'Find boat'.

3. Make sure you know how to call up the depth sounder.
Many screens these days are multifunction and everyone should know how to switch between all the data provided, but for me knowing the depth is always vital, especially in coastal or inshore sailing.

Waypoints

If you don't have a routing program you will enter a waypoint and the plotter will take you in a straight line to the waypoint, regardless of depth of water or hazards.

Here we have entered the waypoints to follow the route from our berth in the Hamble River out to the English Channel by the Needles.

Let's say you are anchored here just off Hook Park and for now you want to go down the road a bit to a waypoint that you have entered into the chart plotter. This example uses iNavX. Move your cursor to the spot, click on it or tap the screen and a waypoint is placed on the chart. If you click on the waypoint you will get the latitude and longitude of this position, its distance from you and the bearing from you to it. If you now click 'Go to' you will see a line from you to the waypoint, in this case in red. And if you set off for the waypoint you will begin to see a number of lines.

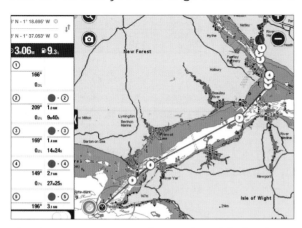

▲ *Nine waypoints entered manually and the bearing and distance from one to another shown.*

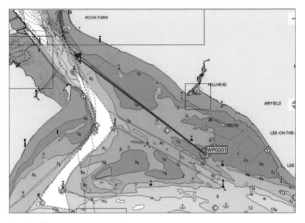

▲ *Sailing to a waypoint.*

Assuming that you have the option to have your route track on, you will see a dotted grey line of your progress stretching out behind your boat back to your start position. You will have a line projecting from the bow of the boat, your heading, yellow in this case. You will have another line showing the direction you need to travel in order to arrive at the waypoint, here in blue, and finally the line that ran from you to your waypoint, in red. Here is a good example of all of those lines:

What is happening in the picture (right) is that the boat is being affected by the tide. You can see how much it is being pushed off course. The blue line is the course you need to steer to reach your waypoint. You need to turn the boat to counter the effect of the tide.

Back from when you were anchored to your first waypoint, you have:

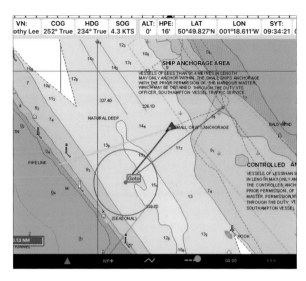

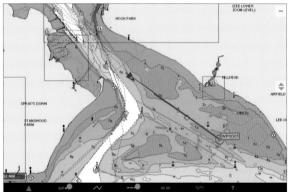

▲ *Heading, course to steer to waypoint, your track, bearing line from your start point to the waypoint.*

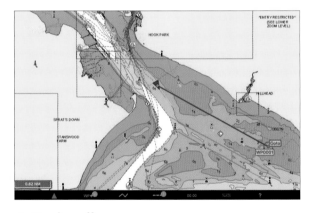

▲ *Heading off course.*

▲ *Heading on course.*

All modern chart plotters, programs and apps combine a number of different data sources, including tide and wind, and are capable of giving you a course to steer from your position to your destination to counter the effect of the tide and the wind. Some chart plotters will do this for you and some shy away from doing this on the basis that they are now beginning to take responsibility for your navigation.

You must remember that every skipper or captain or master is ultimately responsible for their vessel and crew. Regardless of whether a computer advised them to take a certain route, if they should come to grief by following this route they are responsible.

There are chart plotters that will show you the bearing to your destination and how much you are off course and by how much you need to correct this. Other chart plotters will give you a course to steer to stay on the bearing line to your destination and you can get the chart plotter to drive the autohelm to make sure you stay on that line.

Of course, you can work out a course to steer yourself on a paper chart to run directly down the bearing line to your destination and I will show you how to do that in Chapter 12, Course to Steer.

GPS ACCURACY

Everything to do with GPS is based on time, so the accuracy of the clock inside your GPS receiver dictates its initial accuracy in presenting your position. And generally this will be to within 10 metres.

There are also a number of errors that can affect the time taken for the signal to reach you:

- Delays to the signal as it passes through the atmosphere
- Shading (satellites are too close together)
- Satellite position reporting errors
- Signal multipath, where the signal bounces off buildings or land features and therefore takes longer to get to you.

These can be ironed out by a process known as 'augmentation'. This compares the satellite position the GPS has calculated with the satellite position of a known object and provides your receiver with an offset to improve the position accuracy of your GPS set to within 2 metres. The two augmentation systems your GPS sets use are:

1. Differential GPS, which transmits error corrections from land-based features on AM radio;

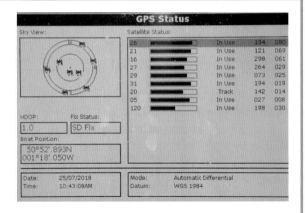

▲ DOP of 1.0. Very good.

2. Wide Area Augmentation System, which transmits error corrections from geostationary satellites.

You can tell how accurate your GPS is by looking at the Horizontal Dilution of Precision (HDOP, sometimes referred to as DOP or HDP). Without getting too technical, if this is reading 2.0 or less then the positional accuracy of your GPS is spot on. If it is reading above 6.0 then it is not reading so accurately. The GNSS (Global Navigation Satellite System) settings on the chart plotter will tell you the accuracy in feet/metres.

Autohelm

The autohelm is linked to the rudder and, as the name suggests, allows the boat to be helmed automatically. It will have at its heart a fluxgate compass. Click from 'Standby' to 'Auto' and it will take over the helm. You can adjust the course as you go, or you can get the chart plotter to control the autohelm.

Route

You can plan a route to follow from one waypoint to another.

A chart plotter used manually (where you input the waypoints and create a route, as opposed to using a 'Dock to Dock' program) will give you a

▲ Autohelm steering the boat to the next waypoint.

straight line to follow, a bearing line directly from you to the waypoint. And it may well be that you cannot go straight to your destination. You may have to navigate round an island or obstruction or via a channel, or over shallows. And so you will need to place waypoints in safe locations.

As each chart plotter is slightly different, you will need to check with the manual exactly how you create a waypoint and how you set up a route.

Now when you press 'Go' on the route, the chart plotter, which is linked to the autohelm, will navigate you to the first waypoint. Well, it will aim the boat directly down the bearing line. If the boat experiences any cross tide and is knocked off course, the chart plotter will continue to aim at the waypoint and eventually you may well find, if you do not correct the course, that the boat is pointing from downtide up towards the waypoint.

Some programs will automatically execute turns when each waypoint is reached, most will not. However, they will alert you when the boat gets to the waypoint and you then press the button to get the plotter and thus autohelm to head for the next waypoint.

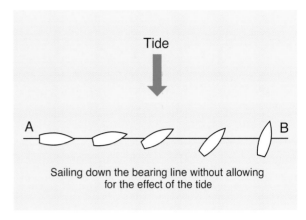

Tide

A _____ B

Sailing down the bearing line without allowing for the effect of the tide

▲ *GPS taking you to the destination without allowing for the tide.*

So you have met the chart plotter and discovered how it can help you.

But you will notice there is a great deal of detail on the chart plotter screen: symbols, numbers, lines, information that is crucial to your safe passage.

When you move from the 'on screen' theory to the 'visual reality' of the thing, you need to know what the chart in the chart plotter is telling you.

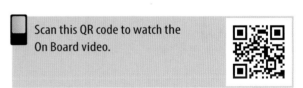

Scan this QR code to watch the On Board video.

3 The chart

To understand what the chart in your chart plotter is telling you, it is necessary to look at the paper chart from which it is derived.

The Falmouth to Plymouth chart tells us that depths are in metres and that the scale is 1:75,000.

A large-scale chart of 1:25,000 will cover a small area and a small-scale chart of 1:500,000 will cover a large area.

ENGLAND — SOUTH COAST

FALMOUTH TO PLYMOUTH

DEPTHS IN METRES

SCALE 1: 75 000 at lat 50°30′

1 **Depths** are in metres and are reduced to Chart Datum, which is approximately the level of Lowest Astronomical Tide.

2 **Heights** are in metres. Underlined figures are drying heights above Chart Datum. Vertical clearance heights are above Highest Astronomical Tide. All other heights are above Mean High Water Springs.

3 **Positions** are referred to the WGS84 compatible datum, European Terrestrial Reference System 1989 Datum.

Navigational marks: IALA Maritime Buoyage System – Region A (Red to port). **4**

Projection: Mercator. **5**

Sources: See Source Diagram. See The Mariner's Handbook for **6** information on Source and Zones of Confidence (ZOCs) Diagrams. The topography is derived chiefly from Ordnance Survey maps.

▲ *Chart title and marginal notes.*

1. Depths

Soundings are in metres. The chart datum here is approximately the level of lowest astronomical tide (LAT). That is the least depth of water you can reasonably expect and you add your height of tide to this to get the depth of water.

2. Heights

Heights are taken to three different levels:

Drying height – this is something that covers and uncovers with the tide, a sandbank, the beach, a rock, and is measured above chart datum with a line under the metres figure.

Vertical clearance height – is the height of a bridge or span and is taken to the highest astronomical tide, the highest tide possible, the worst case.

Mean High Water Springs (MHWS) – is the average height of the spring high water tides. Heights of rocks and charted marks like lighthouses, monuments, towers are measured to this level.

A rock will be shown on a paper chart as a dot with its height above MHWS written in brackets.

A light will be shown on a chart with its light sequence, then its height above MHWS and then possibly its notional visibility in miles on a clear night.

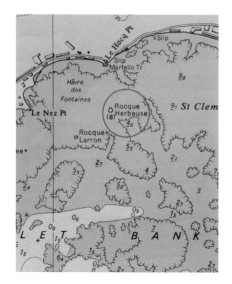

▲ *Rocque Herbeuse is 8 metres above MHWS.*

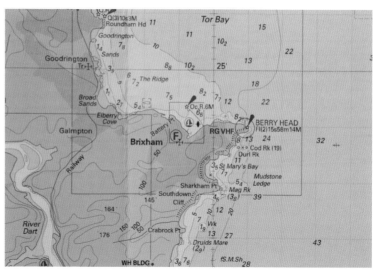

▲ *Berry Head lighthouse FL(2)15s58m14M, meaning Flashing twice every 15 seconds, 58m above MWHS and visible nominally for 14 miles at night. As the light colour is not specified, it will be white.*

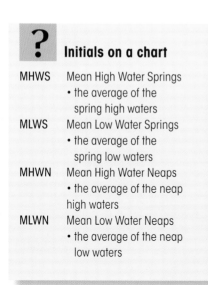

? **Initials on a chart**

MHWS	Mean High Water Springs • the average of the spring high waters
MLWS	Mean Low Water Springs • the average of the spring low waters
MHWN	Mean High Water Neaps • the average of the neap high waters
MLWN	Mean Low Water Neaps • the average of the neap low waters

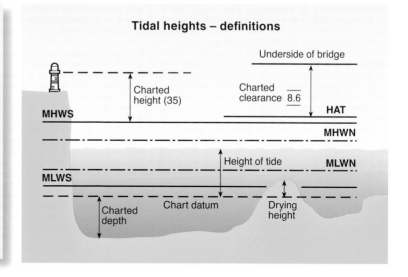

3. Positions

These are referred to WGS84, which is a worldwide standard, and ETRS89, which is a European standard. As long as your chart plotter is reading one of these datums then positions on the chart plotter can be transferred to the paper chart.

4. Navigational marks

This chart follows the International Association of Lighthouse Authorities (IALA) System A, where the port-hand marker is red.

5. Projection

This is a Mercator projection chart. For more on projections, see Chapter 4, Position.

6. Source data

The source data tells you when the surveys were conducted and how accurate the information on the chart might be. Modern-day surveys are conducted with multibeam scanners that can see every inch of what's down there. With lead line surveys of old, while the soundings would be fine they wouldn't necessarily know if there was anything between the soundings. Today's scanners do know and modern charts give you high levels of accuracy. In addition, the marginal notes give you further information about firing practice areas, underwater cables, oyster beds, wrecks, a wave test area and vessel reporting.

A word about accuracy

Your GPS will give you a latitude and longitude position to within 2 metres.

Bearing in mind that a pencil line on a paper chart is about 1mm (a line on a chart plotter may be a little more than this), if you have a chart with a scale of 1:150,000 that makes your 1mm line the equivalent of 150 metres.

So it is impossible to represent this 2m accuracy on a paper or digital chart.

THE CHART IN YOUR CHART PLOTTER

How did the chart get into your chart plotter? There are two types of digital chart:

1. Raster chart

This is simply a digital copy of the paper chart. You can zoom in and zoom out, but the information never changes. You cannot interrogate the information. It is exactly like a paper chart, although on Imray Navigator and NV charts (the German app), where a larger-scale chart for the area is available, as you zoom in on the small-scale chart, the plotter will bring up the larger-scale chart underneath.

▼ *Meridian Chartware's SeaTrak – raster chart.*

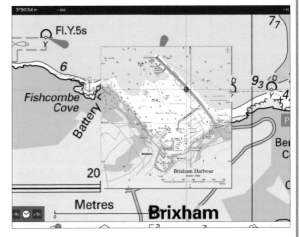

▲ *Small-scale raster chart of Brixham area zoomed in, showing the large-scale chart of the port underneath.*

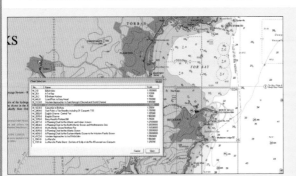

▲ Click on the small-scale chart and select from the available charts …
a large-scale chart to navigate into the harbour ▶

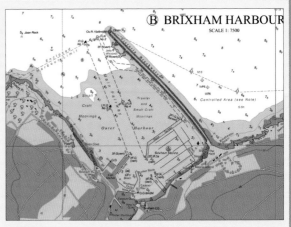

Other raster charts handle this in different ways. For example, Meridian Chartware's SeaTrak on a right click offers you the large-scale charts in the area from which you can choose, which works well.

Where there is no large-scale chart underneath a small-scale chart, you lose focus as you zoom in.

2. Vector chart

This is a layered chart. You can zoom in and zoom out, but you can also change the level of data that you see. For example, if you are crossing a body of water, the Channel, Bass Straight, Mediterranean, Chesapeake Bay, you don't necessarily want a mass of soundings to show up on the chart. But as you approach a port you do want to see the soundings and also every single lateral mark. So you can choose the level of detail you want. Some chart plotters do this automatically.

On a vector chart you will see the symbol for the charted mark and then click on it or hover over it to get the detail – depending on whether you are using a touch screen or a standard LCD screen.

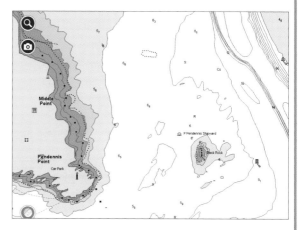

▲ *Vector chart.*

When zoomed out it is possible for hazards not to show up on a vector chart (where they would show up on a paper chart and a raster chart), but when you place a waypoint, as a prudent skipper you would naturally zoom in on the vector chart to make sure that all was well with following that course.

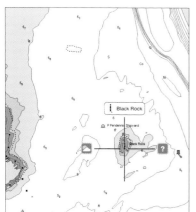

▲ *Black Rock Isolated Danger Mark (IDM).*

▲ *Touch on it for more detail.*

▲ *Touch again to get the detail of the IDM and its light.*

On chart plotters with a 'Dock to Dock' facility, or where you can input desired under keel clearance, even if when zoomed out a hazard did not show up, the Dock to Dock would warn you of any danger and, of course, you would check the route offered.

How atmospheric conditions affect the depth of water

As an aside, it is worth considering that atmospheric conditions, pressure and wind, can have quite an effect on the depth of water. High pressure, for example, can push the water level down and low pressure can allow it to rise. And wind direction and strength can alter the level of water, too.

Ports publish tables to show the effect of atmospheric pressure. But unless you are a marine pilot navigating a deep draught oil tanker in a shallow channel, this is unlikely to worry you. It does, however, explain why the sea can breach our shore-based defences on stormy days in certain parts of the country. Storms equal low pressure, so the water level is a little higher than normal and if this coincides with a very high spring tide and the wind is blowing the sea on to the shore, this can be enough to produce spectacular photo opportunities for the TV crews and misery for the locals.

? Backing up with a paper chart?

ECDIS (Electronic Chart Display and Information System), the charting system used on big ships, is now considered to be so reliable that as long as a ship has two independent ECDIS systems powered by separate Uninterrupted Power Units then they do not need to carry a paper chart.

If I am going offshore I will always run a paper back-up to the electronic chart plotter. *Dorothy Lee* has a nice flat shelf in the cockpit where I keep the paper chart under a piece of perspex.

I plot my position every hour, taken from the GPS. Along with position, I take a note of the time, speed over ground, course over ground, heading, wind direction, wind strength and pressure. There's not much else to do on passage so you might as well fill out the log.

That way, if anything goes wrong with the electronics (unlikely), you will only ever be at most an hour from your last position. For me, that will be no more than 6 nautical miles. For my friend in the Princess 23M, this could be up to 35 miles.

▶ (top) *A depth on a chart plotter of 13.1 metres. Add the height of tide to this to get the depth of water.*

▶ (bottom) *A drying height of 1.3m. If the height of tide was 3m then the depth of water over the drying height would be 1.7m.*

i Differences in chart datum

Not all cartographers use the lowest astronomic tide as the chart datum. NOAA (National Oceanic and Atmospheric Administration) in the USA, for example, uses Mean Lowest Low Water (MLLW), which is a slightly higher datum than LAT. To get the depth of water here you need to make sure that the tide table is giving heights in relation to MLLW. In the Baltic there is so little tide – a few centimetres – that the datum is taken to Mean Sea Level.

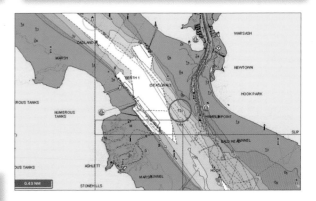

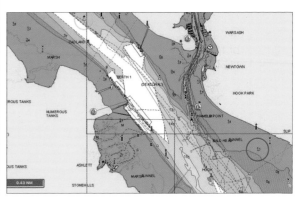

Different chart makers use different colours for:

Land that which is never covered with water
Sea that which never dries
Drying heights which cover and uncover with the tide.

Admiralty Charts show land as buff, drying heights green and water indicating depth from dark blue to white.

Imray chart land is green, drying heights sand coloured, water white to blue.

Stanfords chart land is white, drying heights buff, water white to blue.

There is a wealth of information on a chart, including lateral buoyage, cardinal marks, isolated danger marks, special marks and emergency wreck marking beacons, sector lights, lighthouses, light vessels and direction of buoyage. These will be covered under 'Aids to navigation' in Chapter 17.

In the meantime, there are many charted marks on a chart from monuments to church spires, chimneys, houses, piers, docks, harbours that you can use when navigating close to the shore.

Seabed

The nature of the seabed is written on paper charts and it will be on the raster equivalent. It may or may not be available on a vector chart, depending on the supplier and the location.

These are all seabeds that are good for anchoring in:

M	Mud
P	Pebbles
S	Sand further described as **cS** = coarse sand or **fS** = fine sand
Sh	Shells
bkSh	Broken shells.

This is not so good:

R	Rock

Chart 5011 is a book that gives you the code to everything you will find on a paper chart.

Measuring to and from a charted mark

There is a small circle at the base of every buoy or charted mark and this is the point from which or to which you measure distance or bearing on a paper chart. There are a few exceptions to this, such as church towers or spires where you measure to the cross.

Rocks, Wrecks, Obstructions **IK**

16			Coral reef which is always covered.		421.5 010
17			Breakers		423.2 025
d			Discoloured water	Discol	†Discold 434.6 09

	Plane of Reference for Depths →IH	Historic Wreck →IN		Wrecks
20		On large-scale charts, wreck does not cover, height above height datum		422.1 011
21		On large-scale charts, wreck which covers and uncovers, height above Chart Datum		422.1
22		On large-scale charts, submerged wreck, depth known		422.1 015
23		On large-scale charts, submerged wreck, depth unknown		422.1
24		Wreck showing any part of hull or superstructure at the level of Chart Datum		422.1 011 013a
25		Wreck of which the mast(s) only are visible at Chart Datum		422.2 012
26		Wreck over which the depth has been obtained by sounding but not by wire sweep		422.4 015
27		Wreck over which has been swept by wire to the depth shown		422.3 015a
28		Wreck, depth unknown, which is considered dangerous to surface navigation	On modern Admiralty charts, this symbol is used when the depth over the wreck is thought to be 28 metres (15 fathoms) or less. The limiting depth at which a wreck is categorised "dangerous" was changed from 8 to 10 fathoms in 1960, to 11 fathoms in 1963 and 15 fathoms/28 metres in 1968.	422.5 014
29		Wreck, depth unknown, which is not considered dangerous to surface navigation	On modern Admiralty charts, this symbol is used when the depth over the wreck is thought to be more than 28 metres (15 fathoms) [see IK 28 above for previous depth limits] OR when the depth over the wreck is thought to be 28 metres or less, but the wreck is not considered dangerous to surface vessels capable of navigating in the vicinity	422.6 016
30		Wreck over which the exact depth is unknown, but which is considered to have a safe clearance at the depth shown		422.7
31		Remains of a wreck, or other foul area, no longer dangerous to surface navigation, but to be avoided by vessels anchoring, trawling, etc	Foul †Foul 22 Foul (Where depth known)	422.8 017 029c

▲ *A page from Chart 5011.*

 Scan this QR code to watch a video on the chart.

Rocks, wrecks and obstructions

There are four types of rock that you need to know about. I call this the 1 to 4 of rocks:

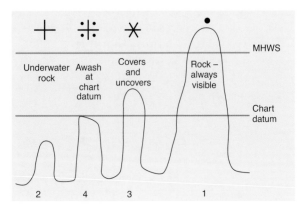

▲ *Four types of rock.*

One	1 dot	One word	1
	• (6)	Rock	
Two	2 lines	Two words	2
	+	Underwater rock	
Three	3 lines	Three words	3
	✱	Covers and uncovers	
Four	4 dots	Four words	4
	⁘	Awash at chart datum	

▲ *How to remember rocks.*

Here are a couple of symbols for wrecks:

Scan this QR code to watch a video on rocks, wrecks and obstructions.

▲ *These wrecks have been swept by wire. Superstructure or masts have been removed and this is the exact depth of the top of the wreck below chart datum. Both wrecks have dots around them, indicating that they are a danger to surface navigation – trawlers and fishermen would want to know about them. The one coloured blue warns that the depth is less than you would expect for the area of depth contour in which it is lying. It should be within the blue 5m contour but is obviously beyond it.*

▶ *The depth of this obstruction has been obtained by sounding.*

▶ *The depth of this wreck is unknown, but there is a safe clearance at the depth shown.*

Updating

A paper chart will have its edition number and date of issue written on the bottom left. To the right of this it will list the updates that have been added to the chart. These Notices To Mariners are issued by the Admiralty and can be found on the internet.

Charts need to be kept up to date as sand banks move, rivers and ports silt up and get dredged, channels can change and buoys are set to mark the area.

To mark an update on a paper chart it is traditional to use a magenta pen.

Updating electronic charts can be done online or by taking a chart dongle or SD card to certain chandlers. Be aware that older chart plotters may need a software update to be able to read the new data on the card. Most modern chart plotters will update charts automatically if you are online.

You can check the date of the digital charts by looking in 'Settings' on the chart plotter.

If you have an old chart plotter and have not updated the charts, do be careful. A chart plotter with maps dating from 2005 will give only sketchy information on light sequences. In the example (right), there is a south cardinal, which, as we all know, has six short flashes and one long flash and that is what is written on the paper chart. Yet when interrogating this, the chart plotter simply says group flashing and long flashing. This plotter needs updating. Worse still, it is one of mine! Good thing I always run a paper plot.

There is a host of useful publications, such as pilot books, tidal stream atlases, sailing instructions, lists of lights and signals, to help you navigate safely.

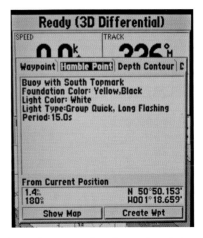

▲ *This chart plotter needs to be updated. Newer software will give the correct light sequence of six short and one long flash.*

Short distances and long distances

The Mercator projection – the rhumb line, where the rhumb line cuts the lines of meridian at the same angle – route is good for sailing relatively short distances.

If you want to sail long distances around the globe, you need to use great circle routes. Take a globe and stretch a piece of string from your position to your destination and it will show you the great circle route – the most direct route to your destination.

You can represent this on a gnomonic chart, where the meridian lines converge at the poles and lines of latitude are drawn as arcs, where any two points on a line of latitude represent a great circle, which is the shortest route.

But to sail this route you would need to keep adjusting the course the whole time.

So what you do is make waypoints along your great circle route a few hundred miles apart and then transfer these to a Mercator projection chart and sail in straight lines from one waypoint to another.

You need to take care when plotting your course as a great circle route, certainly when going east to west or vice versa, will track north of the rhumb line. This could lead you into danger.

The saving between a great circle and a rhumb line route in terms of distance can vary.

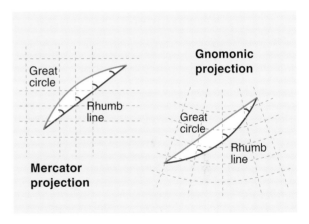

▲ *Rhumb line v great circle.*

For example, in the case of Melbourne to Cape Town the great circle route is 600 miles shorter than the rhumb line. From New York to Cape Town it is just 48 miles shorter.

A GPS will always give you the great circle route – measure the bearing from London to Rio de Janeiro in an atlas and you will get about 205°. Measure it on a chart plotter and you will get 242°. Some plotters also give you the rhumb line route and some give you the composite sailing route. You need to plot this on a Mercator chart just to check that you are not going to hit anything and that the route is good to sail.

Courses (GC)

Great Circle Theoretical Departure Course   `265°`
Great Circle Theoretical Arrival Course   `224°`

The period of the geodetic curve is 359°.2201

Composite Sailing

No

Name	Latitude	Longitude	Course	Dist.	Tot.Dist.	Dist.to go
Start of GC	49°41'.8 N	005°37'.0 W	265°	15.0	0.0	3466.3
Intermediate point	49°40'.4 N	006°00'.0 W	261°	399.1	15.0	3451.3
Intermediate point	48°36'.7 N	016°00'.0 W	253°	423.9	414.1	3052.2
Intermediate point	46°34'.9 N	026°00'.0 W	246°	465.7	838.0	2628.3
Intermediate point	43°25'.8 N	036°00'.0 W	239°	527.3	1303.6	2162.7
Intermediate point	38°55'.5 N	046°00'.0 W	233°	610.8	1830.9	1635.4
Intermediate point	32°46'.7 N	056°00'.0 W	228°	713.9	2441.7	1024.6
Intermediate point	24°43'.4 N	066°00'.0 W	224°	310.6	3155.6	310.6
End of GC	21°01'.0 N	069°55'.7 W	000°	0.0	3466.3	0.0

with reference ellipsoid   `WGS 1984 - 1/298.257223560493`

Lat/Long accuracy (fraction of minute)   `0.1-0.9`

Course accuracy   `000-359`

Distance accuracy   `0.1-0.9`

◀ *From Land's End to the Caribbean, the composite route, changing course every 10° of longitude. Now plot this on a Mercator projection chart to check that the route is safe.*

Maps and charts

We have road maps.
We have weather maps.
But we have navigational charts (although some apps do refer to them as maps).

4 Position

This chapter will cover finding the position of something that is marked on the chart and plotting your position on the chart.

The chart plotter makes it very easy; finding the position of something on the electronic chart is simply a matter of placing the cursor over it...

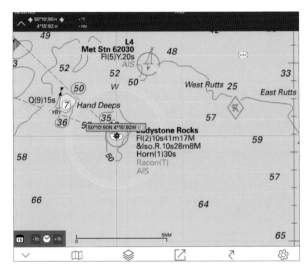

▲ *Put the cursor over Eddystone Lighthouse on Imray Navigator and you get the position on the chart and in the top left-hand corner as you have cursor position selected there. The light sequence is on the chart as this is a raster chart.*

Or clicking on it.

▷ *On a vector chart, iNavX here, you click on the light and drill down to get more information.*

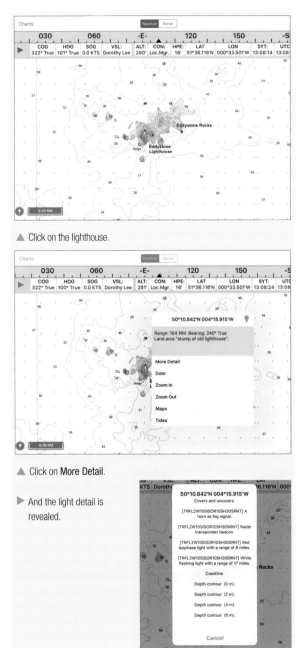

▲ Click on the lighthouse.

▲ Click on **More Detail**.

▷ And the light detail is revealed.

Vector   Raster

▲ *Lat/Long available 24/7 on a chart plotter.*

Plotting a position on an electronic chart plotter is not really a concept you need to understand. The plotter will give you your boat position all the time.

But how does this relate to the paper chart?

It will not have escaped your attention that the Earth is round.

A chart is a flat representation of this. And it is very difficult to make a round shape flat. Gerardus Mercator is the chap who gave us the best representation of the Earth on a flat chart and he did it by 'projecting' this roundness on to a flat surface. If you shone a light through a round globe and captured the reflection on a flat wall you would find that the land round the extremes (the poles) would be splayed out.

Mercator corrected this to a degree, but a chart still does not really represent the true shape of land at the poles. Greenland, for example, is shown as being much wider than it really is. Still, it is good enough for our purposes.

This projection of the round Earth on to the flat paper is called the Mercator projection. Mercator also did a projection where he turned the Earth on its side and projected this on to a flat surface.

This is called transverse Mercator and is more accurate than the standard Mercator projection when dealing with ports and harbours.

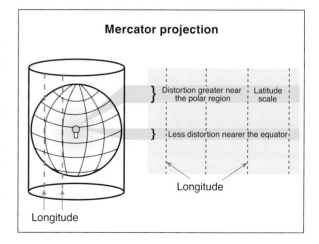

Mercator projection

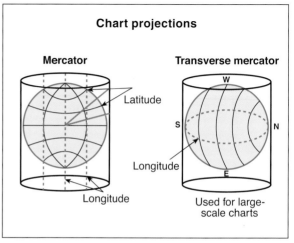

Chart projections

Positions on charts are defined by latitude and longitude.

We have parallels of latitude. These are slices through the centre of the Earth horizontal to the equator. Latitude runs from 0° at the equator to 90° north and 90° south.

We have meridians of longitude. These are slices through the Earth from pole to pole, like a Terry's chocolate orange. And they run from 0° at Greenwich to 180° east and to 180° west.

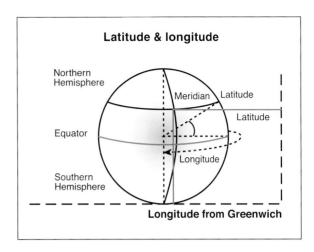

Distance

Distance is measured in nautical miles and tenths of a nautical mile. And it derives from the measurement of the circumference of the Earth at the equator, which is approximately 40,000 kilometres. If you divide this by 360° (the number of degrees in a circle) and then by 60 (the number of minutes in a degree) you come to 1,852 metres. And this is the length of a nautical mile.

If you then divide this by 10, you get to a tenth of a nautical mile (also known as a cable).

You measure distance on the latitude scale and, because of the distortion resulting from the Mercator projection, you measure it beside where you are working on the chart.

You don't measure distance on the longitude scale because one minute on the longitude scale is only ever 1,852 metres on the equator. The distance covered by one minute of longitude decreases as you move from the equator towards either pole.

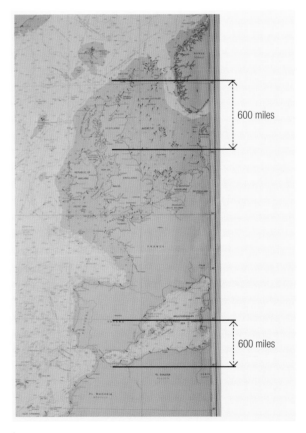

▲ This is why you measure distance on the latitude scale beside where you are working.

Finding the position of something on a paper chart

Here you are in the English Channel and you want to know the latitude and longitude of the lighthouse on Eddystone Rocks.

It is a major light and therefore marked with an unfilled star. The main light is listed as FL(2)10s41m17M, telling you:

FL(2) It flashes twice in the sequence.

10s The sequence is 10 seconds long.

41m The centre of the light (the focal plane) is 41 metres above MHWS.

17M It is nominally visible at night for 17 miles. There is no mention of the colour of the light so it will be white.

There is also another light on this tower, which warns of the danger of the Hands Deeps to the NW of the Eddystone Rocks, and this light is listed as Iso.R.10s28m8M, meaning:

Iso. It is isophase, on as much as it is off.

R. The light is red.

10s The sequence is 10 seconds long so it will be on for 5 seconds and off for 5 seconds.

28m The focal plane of the light is 28 metres above MHWS.

8M It is nominally visible at night for 8 miles.

And there is also a horn, which will sound in fog every 30 seconds.

The lighthouse has a RACON – a radar beacon – which will transmit the Morse letter 'T' (dah – one long), which you would see on your radar if you were within 10 miles of the RACON.

Finally, the lighthouse has an AIS (Automatic Identification System) transmitter and the AIS on your vessel will pick this up.

All this information is also written in the almanac and there you will find the MMSI (Maritime Mobile Service Identity) number of the lighthouse (its unique AIS identification number). You will also find the latitude and longitude of the Eddystone Rocks lighthouse. But no cheating, you're going to find the lat/long from the chart.

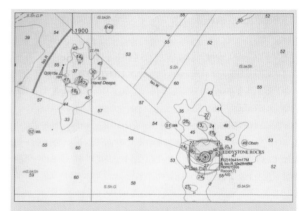

▲ *Eddystone lighthouse.*

❓ What's a RACON?

A radar beacon is a transponder beacon. That is to say, when the radar on your vessel sweeps the horizon it will trigger the RACON to respond. It will transmit a Morse letter and this will show up on your screen in dots and dashes.

▶ *RACON 'T' (dah) from Bridge west cardinal (by the Needles) on your starboard quarter.*

To find the latitude:

▼ **Step 1** With your pencil in the centre of the unfilled star of the lighthouse, bring your plotter up to the pencil. Sliding the plotter so that one of the lines on the plotter lines up with a longitude line (a meridian line), make a mark on the latitude scale to the left. Rather conveniently, on this chart you have latitude scales not just at the far left and right but also two scales running down the centre of the chart.

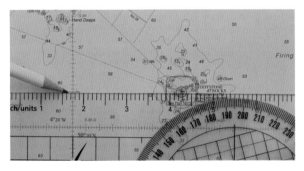

▼ **Step 2** Reading this off, you see that it is 50°10'.85N.

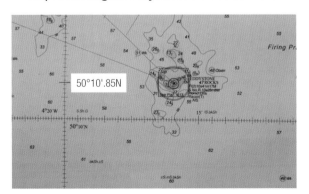

I am using Admiralty Chart 1267 Falmouth to Plymouth.

To find the longitude:

▼ **Step 1** With your pencil in the centre of the unfilled star of the lighthouse, bring your plotter up to the pencil. Making sure that one of the lines on the plotter lines up with a latitude line (a parallel of latitude), make a mark on the longitude scale, which conveniently runs across the chart at this point – you don't need to go to the bottom of the chart to use the longitude scale.

▼ **Step 2** Reading this off, you see that it is 4°15'.9W.

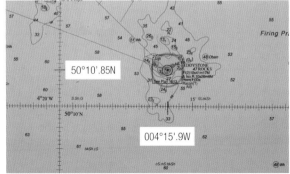

You write this as 004°15'.9W simply for clarity as it is possible to have three digits of longitude to 180°.

It is only possible to have a maximum of two digits of latitude to 90°.

According to you, the lat/long of the Eddystone Rocks lighthouse is: 50°10'.85N by 004°15'.9W.

The difference between the Imray Navigator position as shown on page 29 and your position from the paper chart is probably due to my not centring the cursor exactly over the light on Imray Navigator. Many chart plotters give you the latitude and longitude to the 1/1,000th of a minute, but you couldn't possibly plot this on a paper chart. We need only work to 1/100ths of a minute on a paper chart.

Graticule

Vertical lines of meridian and horizontal lines of latitude are known on a chart as the graticule. Use these to line up your plotter. Also, the surrounds to all information boxes will always be exactly vertical and horizontal and can also be used to line up a plotter.

READ THE SCALE OF THE CHART CAREFULLY

The scale in minutes runs up and down the sides of the chart for the latitude and across the top and bottom of the chart for the longitude. Charts will often have another latitude line running down the middle of the chart and the same for longitude, running across in the centre of the chart.

Depending on the scale of the chart – large scale covers a small area, small scale covers a large area – the intervals within a minute change. On large-scale charts the intervals are likely to be 1/10th of a minute. On smaller-scale charts they may be 2/10ths of a minute. On a chart with a scale of 1:350,000 they will be half a minute.

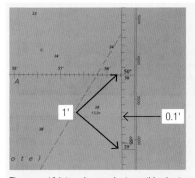

There are 10 intervals per minute on this chart – 1/10th of a minute each

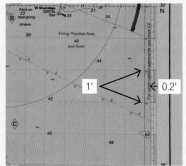

There are 5 intervals per minute on this chart – 2/10th of a minute each

▲ Reading the scale.

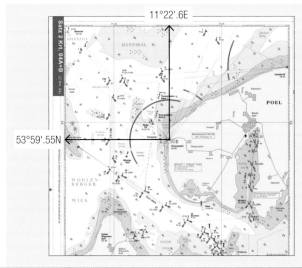

▶ The lat/long of the sector light on Timmendorf on the island of Poel in the German Baltic. Here the latitude scale is in 1/10ths, but the longitude scale is in 2/10ths intervals.

You will notice that I did not draw a line from the lighthouse to the latitude scale or from the lighthouse to the longitude scale but just made marks on the two scales. The reason is that you always rub out your workings at the end of each day or each passage and you don't need acres of line across the charts to have to rub out. It is very important to ensure that you rub out all marks, especially those on the scales, because if you don't, sure as eggs is eggs, when you next come to mark something off on the scale you will mistake what you have just marked off with a mark that was already there and you will end up with the wrong lat or long.

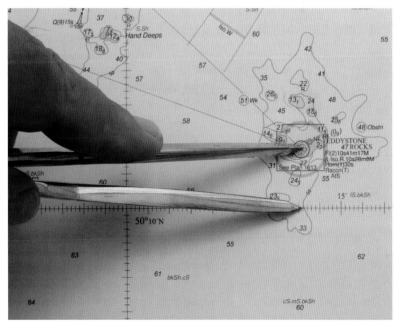

i **Always rub out your workings and route at the end of a passage, except...**

We need to work with clean charts and will rub everything out at the end of a passage. So when a friend of mine went to Trinity House and was shown one of the charts that James Cook had created and he saw that Cook had left his route on the chart, my friend questioned the curator. The curator looked at him a little oddly. 'Well, of course, he left his route on the chart. No one had ever been there and charted the area before and if you follow this route you will be safe.'

You just found a position using your plotter, but the more professional way of doing it is with the dividers. It is also easier with the dividers if you are on a moving boat.

You'll be using the dividers one-handed with the dividers' arms crossed over. Squeezing with the palm of the hand opens them and you use the thumb and forefinger to close them.

▲ Open.

▲ Closed.

▶ **Step 1** Place one end of the dividers into the star at the bottom of the light and the other on a horizontal line running across the chart, here a line of latitude at 50°10'N.

▶ Step 2 Now, keeping the dividers set at this distance, move to the left to the latitude scale running down the middle of the chart and with one end in the 50°10′N mark, read off where the other end comes to – 50°10′.85N.

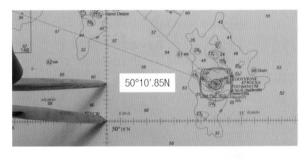

Do the same for the longitude.

▶ Step 3 Stick one end of the dividers into the star at the bottom of the light and the other end on the convenient line to the left running down the chart. Here, a meridian of longitude at 4°20′W.

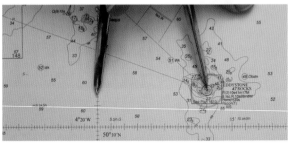

▶ Step 4 Then with the dividers set at this, come down to the longitude scale below and, with one end on the 004°20′W meridian line, where the other end comes to is the longitude of the light – here 004°15′.9W.

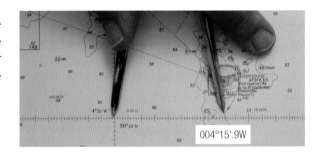

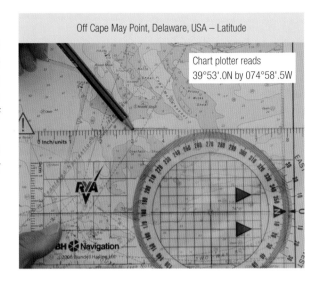

Plotting a position on to a chart

This can be done by using the plotter and working the process in reverse. Find the position on the latitude line. Line the plotter up with the chart and draw a section of line near where the longitude will be. Then find the longitude and make a mark on the section of latitude line you drew.

The GPS told you that you are in position 39°53′.0N by 074°58′.5W just off Cape May Point by Delaware Bay in the good old US of A.

▶ Line the plotter up square with the chart and the 39°53′.0N mark and draw a section of line near longitude 074°58′.5W.

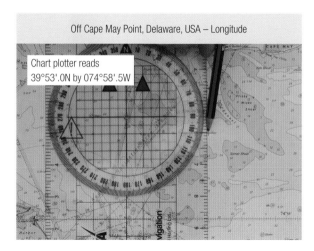

Off Cape May Point, Delaware, USA – Longitude

Chart plotter reads
39°53'.0N by 074°58'.5W

▲ *Plotter lined up on the 074°58'.5W mark on the longitude scale.*

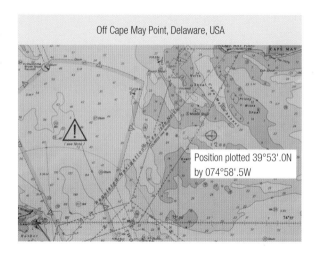

Off Cape May Point, Delaware, USA – Longitude

▲ *Latitude line laid on with the plotter. The longitude line is added with the dividers.*

You cannot actually place a position on a chart entirely with dividers. You always need to make a little section of line along either the latitude or longitude first.

▶ *It is a fix so mark it with a dot with a circle round it and the time, say 1200, and your log reading, say 55 miles.*

Notice how the height of the light on Cape May Point is shown in feet. All the soundings on this chart are also in feet. This is the USA.

Off Cape May Point, Delaware, USA

Position plotted 39°53'.0N
by 074°58'.5W

Bearing and distance from and to

It is much quicker to plot a position on a chart having taken the bearing and distance from a charted mark as shown on the chart plotter than by plotting the latitude and longitude from the chart plotter.

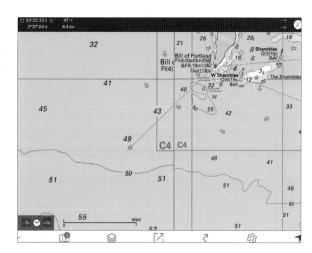

▶ *Bearing and distance from the boat to Portland Bill lighthouse 47°T 8.4 miles.*

▶ *Dial 47° into the plotter, pencil in Portland Bill, line up the plotter with the chart, draw a line back to the boat long enough to measure off 8.4 miles. Job done.*

 Scan this QR code to watch a video on position.

i Reading the chart

You need pin-sharp eyesight to be able to read the tiny detail on a chart. Magnifying glasses with lights can help. Another surprisingly efficient alternative is the range of off-the-peg reading glasses available from high-street chemists, which offer magnification to a variety of degrees. Using these can have the added advantage of leaving both hands free for chart work. (Probably best not to use them for hours on end, or for anything else, as prolonged use may give you a headache.)

▲ *My range of super magnifying glasses.*

5 The compass

There are four types of compass that you come across in marine navigation.

1. Magnetic compass, where the needle points to magnetic north.

A magnetic compass, which gives you readings in degrees magnetic (°M), does not require any power. The steering compass on your boat, whether set into a binnacle or a bulkhead, will be a magnetic compass, as will your hand-bearing compass. You may also have a magnetic compass contained within your binoculars. A magnetic compass is subject to deviation.

▲ *Binnacle compass.*

▲ *Bulkhead compass.*

▲ *Hand-bearing compass.*

2. Fluxgate compass, which measures the Earth's magnetic field.

This requires power. It is subject to magnetic variation, which can be allowed for in its digital readout. It will also be affected by deviation and therefore needs to be sited in a place well away from any magnetic influence on a boat. A fluxgate compass will be driving your autohelm. It can be calibrated to compensate for deviation according to the boat's heading. Readings can be in °T or °M.

▶ *Autohelm compass from the fluxgate compass.*

3. Gyro compass. This requires power. It always finds true north. The needle points to true north. It does not suffer from deviation.

▶ *Gyro compass on a supertanker.*

4. GPS compass. This requires power. It can deliver direction in °T or °M. It does not actually tell you which way you are heading. However, GPS phase change compasses can determine which way the boat is facing.

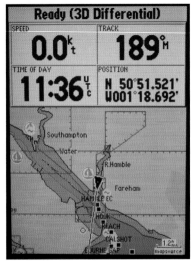

▶ *GPS plotter compass.*

A comparison of compass types

Type	What it does	What it's for	Power?
Magnetic	Points to magnetic north	Steering compass Handheld compass	No
Fluxgate	Measures Earth's magnetic field. Points to magnetic north. Digital. Gives °T or °M, can compensate for deviation	Autopilots	Yes
Gyro	Points to true north. Digital	Steering compass on big ships and ocean-racing yachts	Yes
GPS	Gives heading and course over ground in °T or °M	At the heart of all chart plotters	Yes

6 Magnetic variation and deviation

North on the chart points to true north and all bearings on the chart and in the almanac will be in °T.

However, you take your bearings with a compass and the only compass that doesn't require some form of power is the magnetic compass. So your compass readings will be in °M.

Now, the Earth has its own magnetic field and your magnetic compass will line itself up with magnetic north.

Unfortunately, the magnetic north/south line runs through the Earth at an angle and this causes magnetic north to be in a different place from true north. The actual magnetic north pole lies in the Arctic north of Canada, which is nowhere near true north at the geographic North Pole.

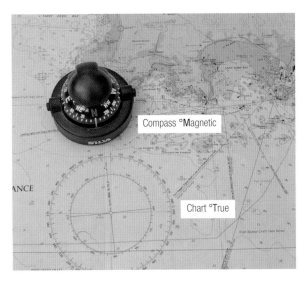

▲ *Magnetic variation.*

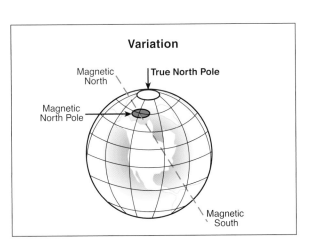

So wherever you are in the world, your magnetic compass needle will point to magnetic north and not to true north. And depending on where you are, magnetic variation, which is the angular difference between true north and magnetic north, will vary between westerly and easterly.

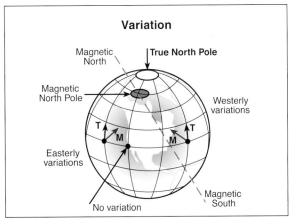

The Earth's magnetic field is complex and the variation you will experience is not simply a question of being to the east or to the west of the north/south magnetic line. Iron ore in the Earth's crust also affects the magnetic field, added to which the Earth's core is melting and solidifying, altering the whole time, the result of which is that the magnetic north pole is on the move. In fact, in a relatively short geological time (about 50,000 years), the poles are due to swap.

In the UK we experience a little westerly variation – according to my Admiralty Charts – from 1°W on the east coast (in 2018) to 3°W on the west coast and this means that when we say we want to travel north up the chart and we ask our magnetic compass to point to north, it says 'certainly' and it will point itself at magnetic north, which if we are off Land's End will be at 357°T and not 360°T. We have to allow for this when taking bearings from the chart in °T and bringing them into °M and vice versa.

What do we do with magnetic variation?

When taking a true bearing from the chart and converting it into magnetic, you add (+) westerly variation and subtract (-) easterly variation.

There are lots of mnemonics and acronyms that people use to remember this, but the one I prefer is simply West is Best, East is Least. When taking a true bearing and converting it into magnetic West is Best, add westerly variation – East is Least, deduct easterly variation.

ESTABLISHING MAGNETIC VARIATION FOR YOUR CHART

All charts will either state what the magnetic variation was at a certain date and how much it has moved annually or they will have a compass rose on which this is written.

On the right is a chart where off the coast of Wales there is a compass rose that gives the magnetic variation in 1998 as 6°W. It has been moving east at 8' every year. If you are in 2018 then it has moved 20 × 8' = 160' or 2°40' east since 1998. So you'll have to take this off the 6° westerly variation to give you 3°20'W variation today. As your compasses only work in whole degrees, round this to the nearest degree. So magnetic variation here in 2018 is 3°W.

Of course, in other parts of the world magnetic variation is considerably greater than in the UK. On the US east coast, variation is around 11° to 12°W; in the Caribbean it is 15°W. In Sydney, Australia, it is 13°E.

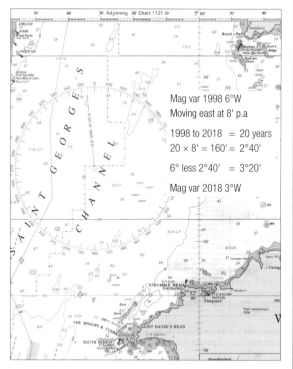

Mag var 1998 6°W
Moving east at 8' p.a

1998 to 2018 = 20 years
20 × 8' = 160' = 2°40'

6° less 2°40' = 3°20'

Mag var 2018 3°W

▲ *Magnetic variation, west coast of England.*

Taking the US east coast with variation of 12°W, a bearing of 090°T from the chart becomes a magnetic bearing of 102°M.

090°T
+12° Westerly mag var
102°M

And the other way, you've just taken the bearing of a charted mark and this is in °M and you want to draw it on the chart, so you need to convert it to °T by taking the westerly variation off.

A magnetic bearing of 314°M with a variation of 12°W becomes a true bearing of 302°T.

314°M
-12° Westerly mag var
302°T

Naturally, where you added westerly variation to a true bearing to get magnetic, you will subtract easterly variation from a true bearing to get magnetic.

In south-east Australia, where variation is 12°E, you take the easterly variation away from the true bearing to get to magnetic:

180°T
-12° Easterly mag var
168°M

And from magnetic to true:

075°M
+12° Easterly mag var
087°T

Here is a diagram to help you. Follow the arrow. If you are starting from true on the left, follow the arrow. If you are starting from magnetic on the right, follow the arrow.

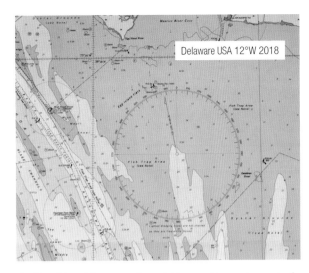

▲ Considerable westerly variation on the east coast of the USA.

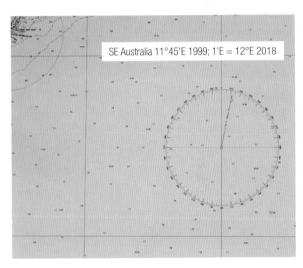

▲ Considerable easterly variation on the south-east coast of Australia.

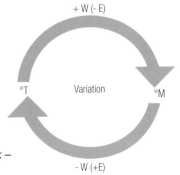

▶ True to magnetic and back – follow the arrow.

ISOGONAL LINES OF THE WORLD

Lines of equal magnetic variation are called isogonal lines.

And this (below) is what magnetic variation throughout the world looks like: Epoch 2015.

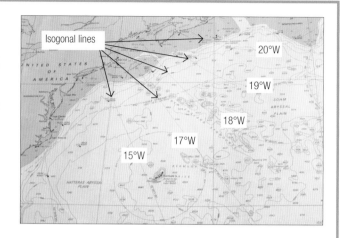

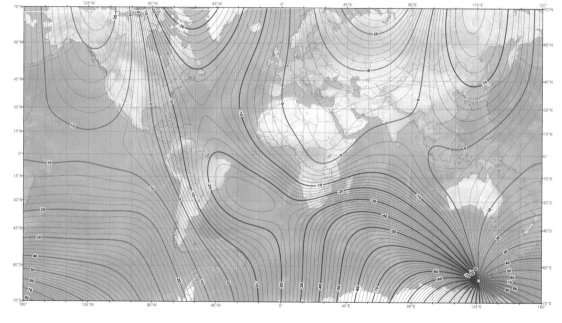

Most chart plotters can give you bearings in °T or °M. Some, Navionics for example, stick with °T, so in that sense they are just like the paper chart, which gives you bearings in °T. Do check what your chart plotter is telling you because if it is giving you °T or the magnetic variation is set incorrectly, what you are being told on the electronic chart will not accord with what you are seeing with your magnetic hand-bearing compass.

Step 1 is to check whether the plotter is giving you °T or °M. If °M and if it has adjusted for this automatically, do check that this is correct. I have come across plotters that have not allowed automatically for the correct magnetic variation. It only really affects things when you try to take information from the chart plotter and plot it on a paper chart. If the paper chart tells you that current mag var is 1°W and the chart plotter is saying 3°W, then when you convert an electronic bearing to °T you will be 2° out with what the bearing should be when written on the chart.

Deviation

This is the effect of local magnetic fields on a magnetic compass – keys, glasses etc.

The degree to which local magnetic fields affect a magnetic compass varies depending on the heading of the boat.

Take a hand-bearing magnetic compass. Turn it so the needle points to north (magnetic north) and then bring a metal object up to it – a penknife, a mobile phone, a set of keys – and see how they affect the needle.

Then turn the compass so the needle is facing east and bring the metal objects up to the compass and see what happens.

Do this for the two other cardinal points of the compass, south and west, and see how the deviation will be significant when the compass is pointing in one or two directions and less so when pointing in the other two.

Always check the deviation when you step on to a new or unknown boat. You'd be surprised how many times there is serious deviation because the owner has added something metal or magnetic next to the magnetic steering compass.

Your steering compass will suffer from deviation to some extent.

Your hand-bearing compass should not.

Steps taken to allow for variation and deviation

Start with a bearing in °T. Convert it first into °M by applying magnetic variation and then into °Compass (°C) by applying deviation to give you a course that the helm will steer:

°T from the chart
+W or -E variation
°M
+W or -E deviation
°C the course the helm will steer

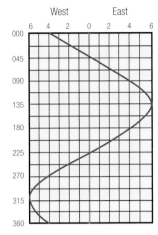

Ship's Head Compass (°C)	Deviation	Ship's Head Magnetic (°M)
000	4W	356
022.5	2W	020.5
045	0	045
067.5	2E	069.5
090	4E	094
112.5	5E	117.5
135	6E	141
157.5	5E	162.5
180	4E	184
202.5	2E	204.5
225	0	225
247.5	2W	245.5
270	4W	266
292.5	5W	287.5
315	6W	309
337.5	5W	332.5
360	4W	356

▲ *Compass deviation table.*

▲ *The fish finder here has recently been added and placed next to the magnetic compass. Deviation on one heading was 47°W. That could be awkward if the navigation electrics went down and you found yourself in fog.*

Going the other way from °C to °T:
°C the course the helm is steering
-W or +E deviation
°M
-W or +E variation
°T the bearing you can draw on the chart

HOW DO YOU CHECK FOR DEVIATION?

Take the magnetic hand-bearing compass and stand away from the steering compass and not near any obvious metal. Ask the helm to steer 000°, then check what the hand-bearing compass reads. If this is greater than 000° then the steering compass has easterly deviation on that heading and if it is less than 000° the steering compass has westerly deviation on that heading. Do this for eight points of the compass – 000°, 045°, 090°, 135°, 180°, 225°, 270°, 335° – and mark down the differences and then make up a deviation curve.

Ideally you should have no more than 2° of deviation on any point of the compass.

Another way of checking deviation is by 'swinging the compass'. That is to say, find a transit (two charted chimneys in line would be good) check the true bearing on a paper chart and convert this to °M, or draw a bearing line on a chart plotter. Make sure the chart plotter bearing is in °M and you know what magnetic variation the chart plotter is working to. Now sail down the transit, check what the steering compass reads. Turn round and sail back along the transit, Then sail across it at right angles in both directions, 090° and 270°. Then sail at 045° and the reciprocal 225° and finally sail at 335° and then 135°. You will have eight headings and the deviation for each and from this you can make up your deviation curve.

To help you move from °T to °M and from °M to °C and vice versa, see the diagram on the right.

Scan this QR code to watch a video on magnetic variation and deviation.

▲ Swinging the compass.

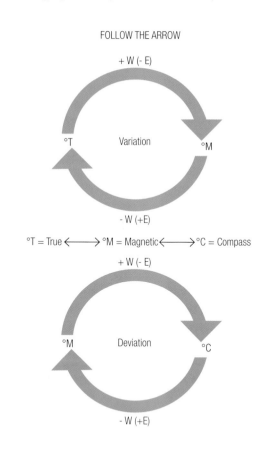

FOLLOW THE ARROW

+ W (- E)

°T   Variation   °M

- W (+E)

°T = True ⟷ °M = Magnetic ⟷ °C = Compass

+ W (- E)

°M   Deviation   °C

- W (+E)

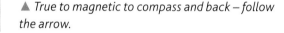

▲ True to magnetic to compass and back – follow the arrow.

7 Fixing a position

You don't need to fix a position on a chart plotter, it gives you your position on the Earth's surface to within 2 metres all day long. That's the beauty of the chart plotter.

Fixing your position from the charted information around you and marking this on a chart takes a little longer.

There are many ways you can fix your position:

1. Charted mark

The easiest way of fixing a position is to place yourself beside a charted mark, a buoy for example.

Mark the position with a dot with a circle round it – the symbol for a fix – and the time beside it and your log reading.

2. Three-point fix

If you are able to identify two charted marks and take the bearings of these and draw them on the chart, where they meet is roughly where you are. If you can identify three charted marks and have three lines of position then where they meet will give you a much more accurate position.

▲ *Bourne Gap port-hand marker.*

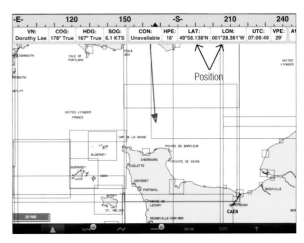

▲ *iNavX chart plotter showing your position.*

Step 1 Find three charted marks that you can identify.

For this three-point fix you are in Stanswood Bay and can clearly see:

- Bourne Gap lateral buoy (port-hand marker) Fl.R.3s (flashing red every three seconds). The magenta (on old charts) or red (on new coloured charts) tear drop tells you it has a light.
- Luttrell Tower
- Outfall ISO.R.10s6m5M &4F.R – which tells you that it is lit with an isophase (on as much as it is off) red light with a sequence length of ten seconds, so it will be on for five seconds and off for five seconds and then it has four fixed red lights around it.

Step 2 With your handheld compass, take the bearing of each:

Luttrell Tower 004°M
Outfall 038°M
Bourne Gap PHM 079°M

Step 3 Convert the bearings from °M to °T

To be able to write these on to the chart, you'll need to convert the bearings to °T. Magnetic variation on this chart in 2018 is just 1°W. As you add westerly variation to °T to bring it into °M, you take westerly variation off °M to bring it back to °T. These bearings in °T therefore become:

Luttrell Tower   003°T
Outfall   037°T
Bourne Gap PHM 078°T

▶ *Luttrell Tower.*

▼ *Outfall.*

▶ **Step 4** Dial the bearing of the first mark, Bourne Gap (78°T), into the plotter.

▼ **Step 5** With a pencil in the charted mark and the plotter lined up with the chart (the central grid of the compass lined up with a vertical or horizontal on the chart and the big arrow on the plotter facing the mark), draw a line from the charted mark towards you.

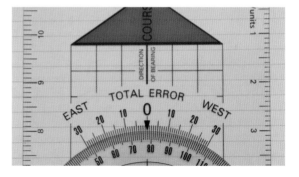

1. 78° dialled into plotter

2. Big red arrow of plotter pointing in direction of Bourne Gap

3. Two red triangles facing north

4. Central grid of plotter lined up with a vertical/meridian line on the chart

Ready to draw in bearing line of Bourne Gap of 78°T

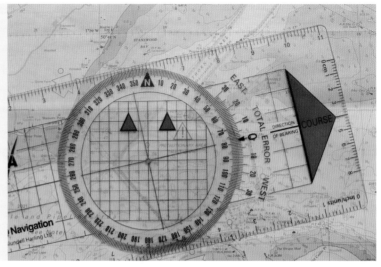

▶ **Step 6** Do this for the next two marks and where all three meet is where you are.

It's a fix, so mark it on the chart with a dot and a circle round it. And the time beside it and the log reading.

To start with you will probably draw the bearing line of each mark in full on the chart, but when you get the hang of rubbing out all your chartwork when you have finished, which you should always do, you quickly realise that the fewer lines on the chart the better. So rather than draw in the entire bearing line from the mark to your position you will just draw the last bit. Just as effective and less to rub out.

In the classroom you always get the three lines to meet exactly. When you are out on a boat this never happens because the boat is moving about a bit and it is hard to get an absolutely accurate reading from a hand-bearing compass, so you end up with a cocked hat.

If you do end up with something of a cocked hat and there is a danger nearby, say a rock, place yourself in the cocked hat near to the danger. Always work to the worst case.

In terms of spread of charted marks, you want them to be even, not too close together and not one on the bow, one on the stern and one on the beam.

And if you're on the move, take any bearing that was on the beam last.

You can always back up the position with a depth.

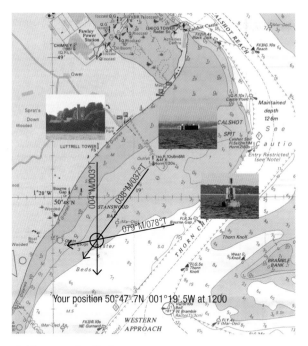

▲ *Three-point fix A.*

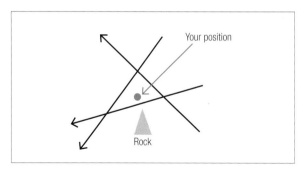

▲ *Cocked hat.*

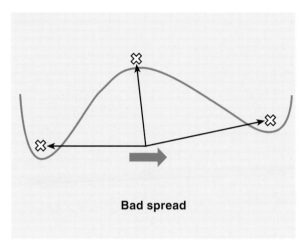

Bad spread

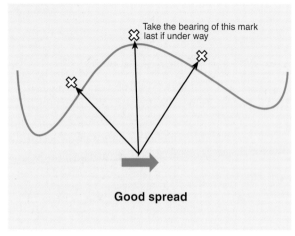

Good spread

3. Single-point bearing and depth

A single bearing on a charted mark doesn't give you much to go on other than to tell you that you are somewhere down that line. However, if you can establish the depth of water and match this to the chart, you can get a reasonable idea of your position.

Here you have taken a bearing on Corbière Lighthouse on the western end of Jersey in the Channel Islands. It bears 134°M. Magnetic variation is 4°W. You have a depth of 14.5m and the height of tide currently is 4.4m. Take this from the 14.5m and you have a 10.1m chart datum sounding. If you are anywhere near that, this will be your position.

Remember that depth of water is chart datum plus the height of tide.

And, believe it or not, the 130°T bearing line on the chart crosses a chart datum sounding of 10.1m. So that is where you are. Well, I set that up, of course, but that is what you do if you only have one charted mark to work with.

Remember to calibrate your depth sound, either to read depth of water or to read depth of water under the keel (under keel clearance). Either is fine, but you need to know which the depth sounder is reading. See Chapter 22 for calibration of the depth sounder.

Bearing 134°M/130°T
Depth 14.5m
Height of tide now 4.4m
Chart datum 10.1m

Position 49°11'.75N 002°16'.6W

CD 10.1m

Mag Var 4°

▲ *Single-point and depth fix.*

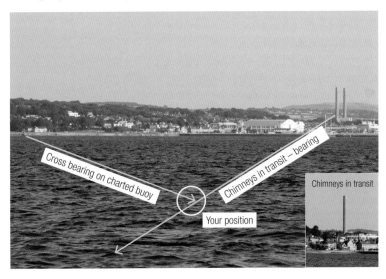

Cross bearing on charted buoy

Chimneys in transit – bearing

Chimneys in transit

Your position

▲ *A fix by 'transit and cross bearing'.*

4. Transit and cross bearing

A transit is formed by two objects being in line. These two chimneys in Cowes when in line form a transit. Draw a line from them on the chart and you are somewhere down this line. If you then add a cross bearing, say to the starboard-hand buoy, and take the bearing of that and plot it on the chart, where the transit and the cross bearing meet is where you are. Again, you can help to confirm this with a depth.

5. Radar range

You need to find three identifiable points on the radar picture that you can relate to the chart.

Measure the distance on the radar to each of these points by using the variable range marker – for greater accuracy, add in the Electronic Bearing Line, so you can pinpoint the edge of the coast or the mark that you were measuring to. Then with a pair of compasses you place one end in the point on the chart and draw an arc back to where you are.

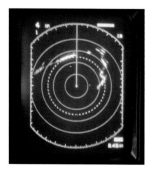

▲ Range 1: 2.45 miles.

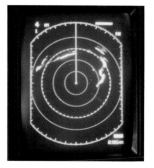

▲ Range 2: 2.95 miles.

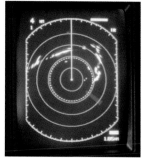

▲ Range 3: 1.85 miles.

▲ Chart plotter position.

▶ The fix by radar range shows the boat to be reasonably close to the actual position from the GPS.

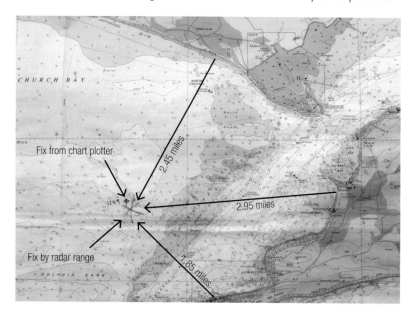

Do this for the other two points and where the three arcs meet is your position.

Again, you can back this up with a depth.

You don't use the bearing line of the radar on its own because the beam of the radar is about 5° wide so the fix is not that accurate.

6. Sector light plus depth

Another way of establishing your position is to use a sector light. As you cross from one sector to another, say from the red to the white, the line of bearing at which these sector lights change colour will be marked on the chart. So you are down this line somewhere. If you can back this up with a depth, you can get an idea of where you are.

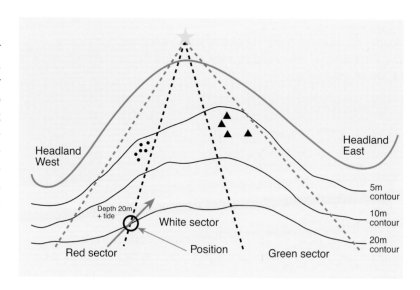

▶ A fix by sector light and depth.

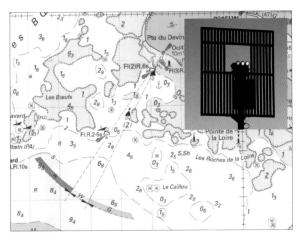

▲ *Sector light.*

7. Doubling the angle on the bow

If you don't have much to go on in terms of charted marks, but say there is a lighthouse on shore ahead, you can take the bearing of this. When it bears 045° relative to the boat note your heading and log reading and then hold a steady course. And when the lighthouse bears 090° relative to the boat, read the log again. If that has increased by, say, 5 miles then you might assume that you are 5 miles distant from the lighthouse as you have just sailed down one leg of an isosceles triangle – two equal sides. And you can plot this position on the chart.

Of course, this doesn't take account of any tide or leeway that might be sweeping you towards the lighthouse and you should treat it with caution. Again, you can improve the quality of your 'fix' with a depth. But if you had nothing else to go on, doubling the angle on the bow would at least give you an idea of where you might be.

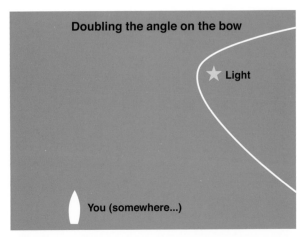

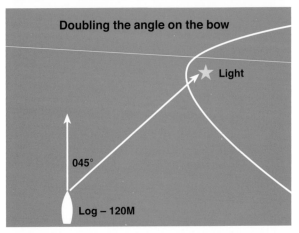

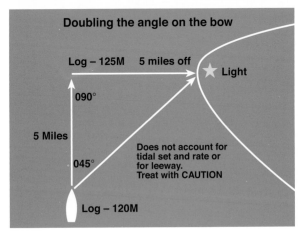

Type of position fix	Quality
By a charted mark	Good
Three-point fix	Best
Single-point fix and depth	Average
Transit and cross bearing	Good
Radar range	Average
Sector light and depth	Average
Doubling the angle on the bow	Poor

8 Tides

The tides are a direct result of the relationship between the Earth, the moon and the sun.

Tides are caused by the gravitational effect of the moon on the Earth. When the moon is close we have a high tide and when it is at right angles to our position we have a low tide. Interestingly, while we are experiencing a high tide on our side of the Earth, they are also experiencing a high tide on the other side of the Earth. The same with the low tide. And this is because the moon is not orbiting a stationary Earth. The Earth and the moon are free-floating objects. They orbit about each other.

Of course, there is another body involved with this and that is the sun. When the sun and moon are in line, the combined effect is increased and we have our highest high tides and lowest low tides. These are called spring tides. When the sun and the moon are at right angles to each other, we have our lowest high tides and highest low tides and these are called neap tides.

At springs we have the highest high tide and the lowest low tide and there is a lot of water coming and going, which gives us our strongest tidal streams. At neaps we have our lowest high tide and our highest low tide and there is less water coming and going and we have weaker tidal streams.

Tides and tide tables can be worked out for years ahead, because we are able to predict the position and movement of the sun, Earth and moon.

Most places have two high tides every 24 hours, which is referred to as semidiurnal. Some places, because the moon does not orbit the Earth directly around the equator, have only one high tide every 24 hours – diurnal. Some places have a double high water, like Southampton, which is caused for some reason by a shallow section in the Channel and has nothing much to do with the Isle of Wight.

? What causes tides?

- The moon is orbiting around a moving Earth
- For an object in space to remain in stable orbit around a host, it must be travelling at a precise speed
- Only the centre of Earth travels at this speed. It maintains the conservation of angular momentum, neither greater than nor less than Escape Velocity
- The side nearest the moon is going slower than this
- The side opposite the moon is going faster than this.

B is travelling at a constant speed to remain in orbit
C slower than B and moon's gravity pulls water towards it
A faster than B, moon's gravity is less and water tries to escape

▲ *The Earth and the moon – gravity versus rotational force.*

The moon itself rotates but only very slowly, going once round in its 29.5-day orbit of the Earth, which means we only ever see one side of the moon.

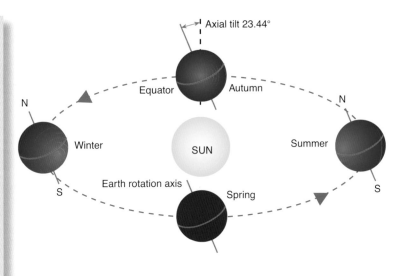

Interesting facts

- Earth is spinning at 1,000mph at the equator.
- Earth travels at 67,000mph to get round the sun in one year.
- Earth is tilted at 23.44° – axial tilt/obliquity of the ecliptic.
- When the northern hemisphere is closer to the sun, we have summer and the southern hemisphere has winter.
- When the southern hemisphere is closer to the sun, they have summer and the northern hemisphere has winter.

▲ Earth orbit around the sun.

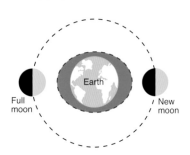

▲ Spring tides.

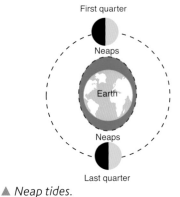

▲ Neap tides.

And as the lunar calendar advances against the Earth's calendar so the time of high water gets later each day. In 24 hours the time of high water is delayed by about 50 minutes. So if high water this morning was 1030, it will be 1120 tomorrow morning. This is not constant as it depends on whether we are at neaps or springs, but on average we can allow 50 minutes.

Spring tides occur when the sun and the moon are in line, with either the moon between Earth and the sun (when we will have a new moon and are unable to see the moon in the sky) or when we are between the sun and the moon (when we will have a full moon and the sun's rays, shining from the other side of the world, light up the surface of the moon for us).

When the moon is at right angles to the sun and has a crescent shape, it's neaps.

More facts

- The moon orbits the Earth every 29.5 days.
- The Earth revolves once every 24 hours.
- Twice within 24 hours we are in line with the moon, either facing it or across the other side of the world from it. At this point we have high water.
- When we are at 90° to the moon we have low water.
- We have two high waters and two low waters every 24 hours. This is known as semidiurnal.

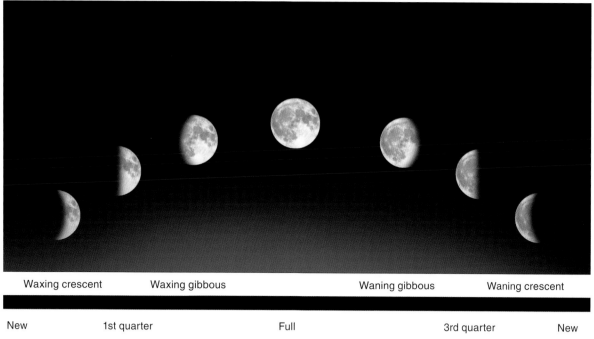

| Waxing crescent | Waxing gibbous | | Waning gibbous | Waning crescent |

| New | 1st quarter | Full | 3rd quarter | New |

| 7 days | 7 days | 7 days | 7 days |

▲ *The phases of the moon, northern hemisphere. The phases from new to first quarter, first quarter to full, full to third quarter, third quarter to new each take just over seven days. This is reversed in the southern hemisphere.*

? Blue Moon

- A lunar month is 29.5 days
- A calendar month is 30.5 days
- At the end of the year the lunar month is ahead of the calendar month by 11 or so days
- After three years it is 33 days ahead and we have two full moons in a month – a Blue Moon – rare.

i Moon phases

Knowing the state of the tide by looking at the moon is very useful. In the northern hemisphere, when you see a 'D' shape in the sky you know the moon is waxing, growing from a new moon (springs) to a full moon (springs). A perfect 'D' indicates a neap tide. And when you see a 'C' shape the moon is waning, reducing from full to new. In the southern hemisphere this is reversed: the moon is 'C' shaped when it waxes and 'D' shaped when it wanes.

When it comes to finding the height of tide, you can use apps or look on the internet and this is what you'll find:

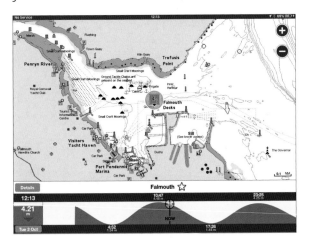

▲ Navionics in app tidal height for Falmouth.

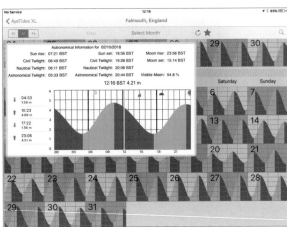

▲ AyeTides tidal height for Falmouth.

Or you can look in the almanac.

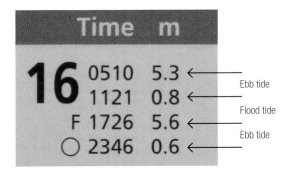

▲ Plymouth tide table (extract), giving the standard time for the port UT/GMT. You need to add one hour to the times in the unshaded areas as this is summer time.

▲ This is Friday 16 September. There is a full moon and these are the times of HW and LW on the day.

No matter where you are in the world, HW springs at your home port will be at the same time +/- 1 hour every time, while neaps will be about 6 hours different, +/- 1 hour, every time:

- In Plymouth, in the UK, HW springs are roughly at 0700 and 1900 and neaps at 0100 and 1300.
- In Sydney, in Australia, HW springs are around 0915 and 2115, with neaps at 0315 and 1515.
- And in Chesapeake Bay, in the USA, HW springs are around 0730 and 1930 and neaps 1330 and 0130.

So when I am at home and I see a full moon, I know the time of high water at my berth – Southampton springs 1200 and 0000 – and if I see a crescent moon I know what the time of high water will be – neaps 0600 and 1800. Anything in between and I will have to make an educated guess and, of course, I always confirm my estimate with the almanac. If I can see the moon, I also know that the pressure is higher rather than lower (clear sky as opposed to overcast) and that tells me that the wind will be more northerly.

Overcast, a low, will give more southerly winds. So I have a great deal of information before I even set off from home, just by looking at the sky.

Tidal hour

Knowing which hour of the tide you are sailing in when using a chart plotter is not especially helpful as the chart plotter will be doing all the clever arithmetic for you and calculating the movement of the tide and updating it as you go along.

But if you are to work out an estimated position or a course to steer on a paper chart, then making sure you are working to the correct tidal hour is extremely important. Get it right and all will be happiness. Get it wrong and misery will result as you find that the set and rate of the tide that you thought you were experiencing or would experience turns out to be quite different in reality as you had based this on the wrong hour of the tide.

And it really is no good shorthanding the simple calculation because the minute we do that we make a mistake. Well, I do, anyway.

Tides come in (flood) and go out (ebb) gradually and the hour of high tide lasts from 30 minutes before high water until 30 minutes after high water and you work your hours of the tide to this.

If HW was 1200, the hour of HW would be 1130 to 1230.

To draw a tidal hour diagram:

Step 1 Draw a line and write 1200 on it and under the line, 'the currency' – UT or DST. Remember, all times in the almanac are in the standard time of the country; for the UK this is UT.

Step 2 Draw a chevron and a line out from each arm and the time of 30 minutes before HW on the top line and 30 minutes after HW on the bottom line and in between HW.

Now you have to decide when you'll be sailing. If this is in the morning you'll be sailing on the flood tide from LW at around 0600 to the 1200 HW and if in the afternoon on the ebb tide from HW at 1200 to LW at 1800 or so.

Let's say you are sailing for an hour at 1530. Which hour of the tide are you sailing on?

Step 3 Extend your hours from 1230, with a chevron and a line and then 1330 written on it and +1 in the gap.

And then another chevron and hour to 1430 and +2 in the gap and then to 1530 and +3 in the gap. Resist the temptation to stop at this point. I know you weren't thinking of stopping because you knew jolly well that you'd be sailing from 1530 to 1630 – one hour – and that you must draw out another hour to 1630 and write +4 in between. But it is a classic classroom mistake. And if you had stopped at 1530 you'd have thought you were sailing in HW+3 when in fact you are sailing in HW+4 and sometimes there can be quite a difference in the direction and rate of the tide from one hour to the next.

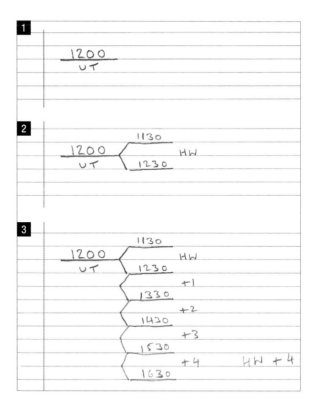

▲ *1200 UT. If it was summer time you would add an hour to this to make it 1300 and put' 'the currency', DST, under the line.*

Working across time zones

Let's say you are having to work across two time zones. You are in France in July, which is on Central European Summer Time (CEST), and the chart of the Channel you are using refers its tidal data to Dover in England. The times in the Dover tide table will be in UT, which is 2 hours different to CEST.

EXAMPLE (WORKING ACROSS TIME ZONES)

It is 28 June, and you want to set sail at 0630 French time. This 0630 CEST.

Step 1 Take 2 hours off the 0630 time to get to 0430 UT.

Step 2 Check the Dover tide table. There is a HW on 28 June at 1117. There is also a HW the day before on 27 June at 2300. Had you not taken the French time back to UT you might have thought that you were sailing on the flood tide on 28 June, with a HW at 1117. But you are not, you are sailing on the ebb tide from the HW at 2300 on 27 June.

Step 3 Add 2 hours to the 2300 UT HW on 27 June to make it 0100 CEST on 28 June.

Step 4 Draw out the tidal hour diagram to discover that you are sailing in the hour of HW+6.

Do it like this every time and you will never come unstuck.

I recommend taking your local French time and converting it into UT by taking 2 hours off it. You then find the HW for the tide you'll be sailing on in the Dover tide table, then add back the 2 hours and draw up your tidal hour diagram as before.

Tidal diamonds and the tidal stream atlas

You don't really have to think about the arrows on the chart plotter, which show the direction and the rate of the tide, because it is all worked out for you. All the tidal information is stored in the chart plotter, times of HW and LW, the heights, the set of the tide (the direction in which it is going), how fast it is running, the rate, all in the machine.

But if you are to work this out for yourself on a paper chart, you have to know where to look and what to look for. Navigation is generally just a matter of knowing where to look to find things.

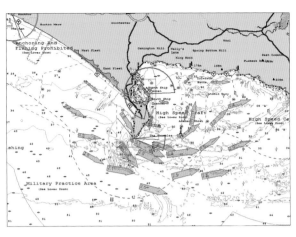

▲ PC Plotter with tidal stream arrows.

Tidal set and rate information is presented to you on a paper chart and in the almanac in two ways:

· as tidal diamonds on the chart
· as a tidal stream atlas in an almanac or a dedicated tidal stream atlas.

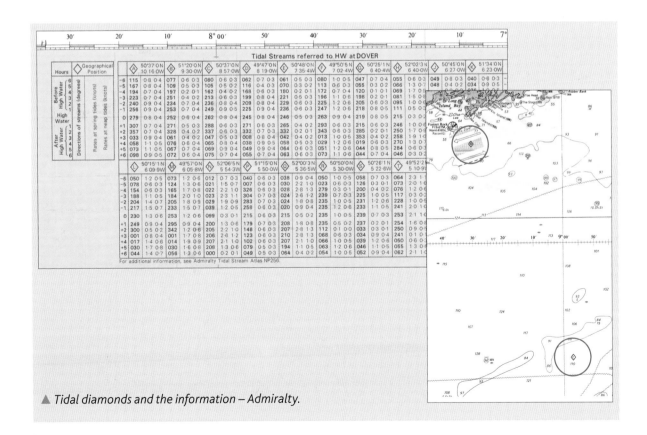

▲ Tidal diamonds and the information – Admiralty.

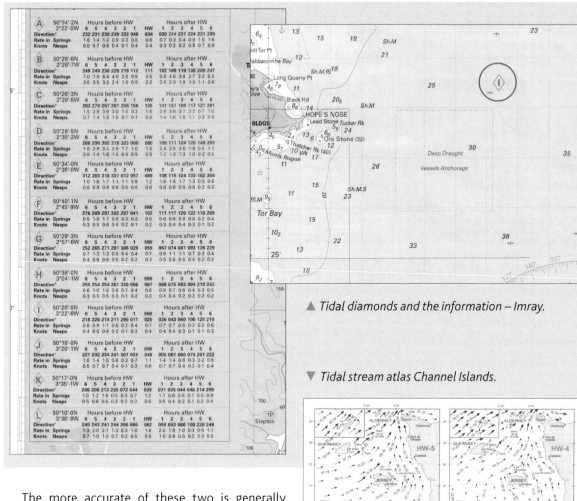

▲ Tidal diamonds and the information – Imray.

▼ Tidal stream atlas Channel Islands.

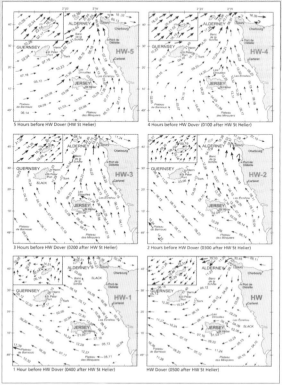

The more accurate of these two is generally the tidal diamond, because someone sat in a boat at a specific location and measured the set (the direction) and the rate (the speed or the rate of drift) of the tide over a huge number of tides to establish what it did every hour during a spring tide with lots of water sloshing about and what it did on a neap tide when there was less water flooding and ebbing. So at that position the tidal information will be very accurate.

A tidal stream atlas is an extrapolation of this data to cover more of the area and is therefore less accurate. That said, there are a number of tidal stream atlases that are very accurate, especially if they have been measured for racing sailors to use, as is the case with Graham Sunderland's *Winning Tides* in the Solent.

Tidal diamonds: how to read the information

Step 1 Find the nearest tidal diamond for the water you'll be sailing through.

Step 2 Find the tidal diamond information on the chart. And check which standard port the tidal streams are referred to.

The fact that you may be nowhere near the port in question, or indeed that the port may not actually be on the chart, doesn't matter. As long as you work to the tide table of the port to which they have referred the tidal diamonds, the information will be accurate no matter where you are on the chart.

Step 3 Find the time of HW for this standard port for the tide that you will be sailing on. Note height of HW and LW.

Step 4 Do a tidal hour diagram to find out the hour of the tide you will be sailing on.

Step 5 Take the LW height from the HW height to establish the range of the tide.

Step 6 Go to the tidal curve for the port in question and see what the mean spring and neap ranges are. At RYA Day Skipper level you only deal with ranges that match springs, neaps or midway.

Step 7 Go to the tidal diamond information on the chart and read off the tidal set for the hour you are sailing on and the rate, depending on whether the range matched the spring or neap range or was midway.

EXAMPLE

It is 0855 on Friday 19 August. You are near tidal diamond N and the tidal diamonds are referred to HW Dover.

▶ **Step 1** Find HW Dover on that day for the tide you will be sailing on.

HW Dover on 19 August is at 1125UT. You'll be sailing on the flood tide.

This is summer time so you add an hour to the UT time to make HW 1225DST. Height of tide at HW is 6.9m. Height of tide at the LW before was 0.9m. The range is 6m, which is spot on the mean spring range.

▶ **Step 2** Do the tidal hour diagram to find that you are sailing on HW-3.

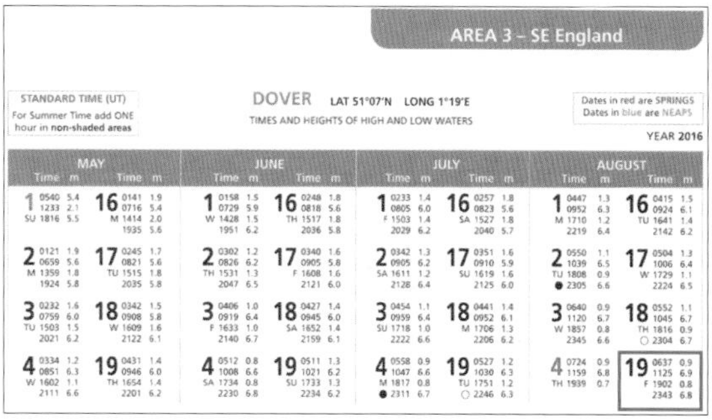

AREA 3 – SE England

STANDARD TIME (UT)
For Summer Time add ONE hour in non-shaded areas

DOVER LAT 51°07'N LONG 1°19'E
TIMES AND HEIGHTS OF HIGH AND LOW WATERS

Dates in red are SPRINGS
Dates in blue are NEAPS

YEAR 2016

	MAY		JUNE		JULY		AUGUST	
	Time m	Time m	Time m	Time m	Time m	Time m	Time m	Time m
	1 0540 5.4 / 1233 2.1 / SU 1816 5.5	**16** 0141 1.9 / 0716 5.4 / 1414 2.0 / 1935 5.6	**1** 0158 1.5 / 0729 5.9 / W 1428 1.5 / 1951 6.2	**16** 0248 1.8 / 0818 5.6 / TH 1517 1.8 / 2036 5.8	**1** 0233 1.4 / 0805 6.0 / F 1503 1.4 / 2029 6.2	**16** 0257 1.8 / 0823 5.6 / SA 1527 1.8 / 2040 5.7	**1** 0447 1.3 / 0952 6.3 / M 1710 1.2 / 2219 6.4	**16** 0415 1.5 / 0924 6.1 / TU 1641 1.4 / 2142 6.2
	2 0121 1.9 / 0659 5.6 / M 1350 1.8 / 1924 5.8	**17** 0245 1.7 / 0821 5.6 / TU 1515 1.8 / 2035 5.8	**2** 0302 1.2 / 0826 6.2 / TH 1531 1.3 / 2047 6.5	**17** 0340 1.6 / 0905 5.8 / F 1608 1.6 / 2121 6.0	**2** 0342 1.3 / 0905 6.2 / SA 1611 1.2 / 2128 6.4	**17** 0351 1.6 / 0910 5.9 / SU 1619 1.6 / 2125 6.0	**2** 0550 1.1 / 1039 6.5 / TU 1808 0.9 / ● 2305 6.6	**17** 0504 1.3 / 1000 6.4 / W 1729 1.1 / 2224 6.5
	3 0232 1.6 / 0759 6.0 / TU 1503 1.5 / 2021 6.2	**18** 0342 1.5 / 0908 5.8 / W 1609 1.6 / 2122 6.1	**3** 0406 1.0 / 0919 6.4 / F 1633 1.0 / 2140 6.7	**18** 0427 1.4 / 0945 6.0 / SA 1652 1.4 / 2159 6.1	**3** 0454 1.1 / 0959 6.4 / SU 1718 1.0 / 2222 6.6	**18** 0441 1.4 / 0952 6.1 / M 1706 1.3 / 2206 6.2	**3** 0640 0.9 / 1120 6.7 / W 1857 0.8 / 2345 6.6	**18** 0552 1.1 / 1045 6.7 / TH 1816 0.9 / ○ 2304 6.7
	4 0334 1.2 / 0851 6.3 / W 1602 1.1 / 2111 6.6	**19** 0431 1.4 / 0946 6.0 / TH 1654 1.4 / 2201 6.2	**4** 0512 0.8 / 1008 6.6 / SA 1734 0.8 / 2230 6.8	**19** 0511 1.3 / 1021 6.2 / SU 1733 1.3 / 2234 6.2	**4** 0558 0.9 / 1047 6.6 / M 1817 0.8 / ● 2311 6.7	**19** 0527 1.2 / 1030 6.3 / TU 1751 1.2 / ○ 2246 6.3	**4** 0724 0.9 / 1159 6.8 / TH 1935 0.9	**19** 0637 0.9 / 1125 6.9 / F 1902 0.8 / 2343 6.8

Handwritten notes:

FRIDAY 19TH AUGUST

HW DOVER 1225 DST
HEIGHT HW 6.9m
LW 0.9m
6.0 SP

0855
    –3   HW–3 SP
0955
    –2
1055
    –1
1155
1225 DST   HW
1255

Continued ▶

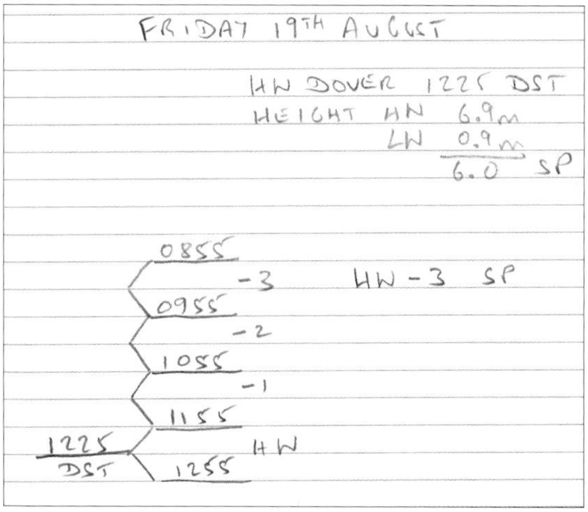

▶ **Step 3** Check the range of 6m against the mean ranges by the tidal curve in the almanac.

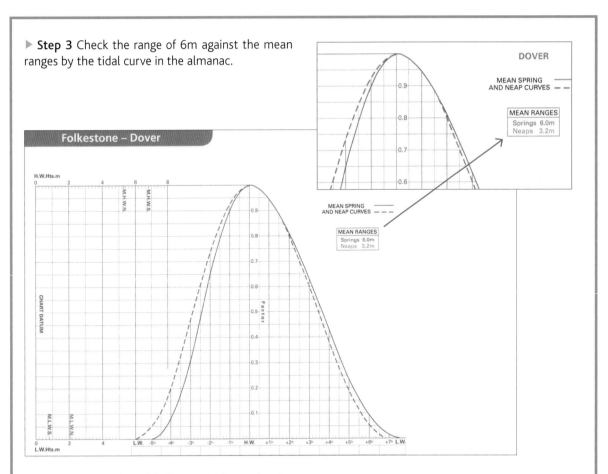

Folkestone – Dover

DOVER

MEAN SPRING AND NEAP CURVES

MEAN RANGES
Springs 6.0m
Neaps 3.2m

▼ **Step 4** Go to the tidal diamond information for N and read off the set and rate for HW-3, which is 023°T 2.3 knots.

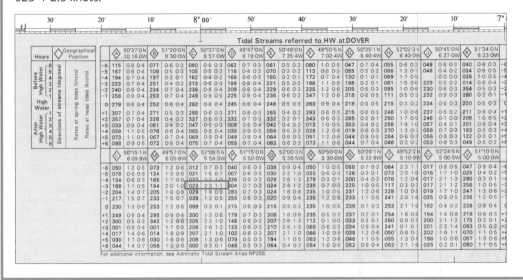

Tidal Streams referred to HW at DOVER

Hours	50°37.0N 10.16.0W	51°20.0N 9.30.0W	50°37.0N 8.57.0W	49°47.0N 8.19.0W	50°48.0N 7.35.4W	49°50.5N 7.02.4W	50°25.1N 6.40.4W	52°02.3N 6.40.0W	50°45.0N 6.27.0W	51°34.0N 6.23.0W
-6	115 0.8 0.4	077 0.6 0.3	080 0.6 0.3	062 0.7 0.3	061 0.5 0.3	080 1.0 0.5	047 0.7 0.4	055 0.6 0.3	049 0.8 0.3	040 0.6 0.3
-5	167 0.8 0.4	109 0.5 0.3	105 0.5 0.2	116 0.4 0.3	070 0.3 0.2	113 0.6 0.3	055 0.3 0.2	066 1.3 0.7	048 0.4 0.2	034 0.9 0.5
-4	194 0.7 0.4	197 0.2 0.1	162 0.4 0.2	168 0.6 0.3	180 0.2 0.1	172 0.7 0.4	120 0.1 0.1	069 1.7 0.9	000 0.0	026 1.0 0.5
-3	223 0.7 0.4	251 0.4 0.2	213 0.6 0.3	199 0.8 0.4	221 0.5 0.3	196 1.1 0.6	198 0.2 0.1	081 1.5 0.8	229 0.5 0.2	014 0.8 0.4
-2	240 0.9 0.4	234 0.7 0.4	236 0.8 0.4	209 0.8 0.4	229 0.6 0.3	225 1.2 0.6	205 0.8 0.3	095 1.0 0.6	230 0.8 0.3	354 0.5 0.3
-1	256 1.0 0.5	253 0.7 0.4	249 0.9 0.5	225 0.9 0.4	236 0.6 0.3	247 1.2 0.6	218 0.8 0.5	111 0.5 0.3	232 0.9 0.3	280 0.2 0.1
0	279 0.8 0.4	252 0.6 0.4	262 0.8 0.4	245 0.8 0.4	246 0.5 0.3	263 0.9 0.4	219 0.8 0.5	215 0.3 0.2	234 0.8 0.3	220 0.5 0.3
+1	307 0.7 0.4	271 0.5 0.3	288 0.6 0.3	271 0.6 0.3	265 0.4 0.2	293 0.6 0.3	215 0.6 0.3	246 1.0 0.6	237 0.5 0.2	211 0.9 0.4
+2	357 0.7 0.4	328 0.4 0.2	337 0.6 0.3	332 0.7 0.3	332 0.2 0.1	343 0.6 0.3	285 0.2 0.1	250 1.7 0.9	246 0.1 0.0	208 1.0 0.5
+3	033 0.9 0.4	061 0.4 0.2	047 0.5 0.3	008 0.8 0.4	042 0.4 0.2	013 1.0 0.5	353 0.4 0.2	258 1.9 1.0	057 0.4 0.1	201 0.9 0.4
+4	058 1.1 0.5	076 0.6 0.4	065 0.8 0.4	038 0.9 0.5	058 0.5 0.3	029 1.2 0.6	019 0.6 0.3	270 1.3 0.7	058 0.7 0.3	183 0.5 0.3
+5	073 1.1 0.5	067 0.7 0.4	069 0.9 0.4	049 0.9 0.4	064 0.6 0.3	051 1.2 0.6	044 0.8 0.5	284 0.6 0.3	056 0.9 0.3	122 0.3 0.1
+6	098 1.0 0.5	072 0.6 0.4	075 0.7 0.4	055 0.7 0.4	063 0.6 0.3	073 1.1 0.6	044 0.7 0.4	046 0.7 0.4	053 0.8 0.3	049 0.5 0.2

Hours	50°15.1N 6.09.9W	49°57.0N 6.05.8W	52°06.5N 5.54.3W	51°15.0N 5.50.0W	52°00.3N 5.36.5W	50°50.0N 5.30.0W	50°26.1N 5.22.6W	49°52.2N 5.10.9W	52°24.5N 5.00.5W	51°10.0N 5.00.0W
-6	050 1.2 0.5	073 1.2 0.6	012 0.7 0.3	040 0.6 0.3	038 0.9 0.4	050 1.0 0.5	058 0.7 0.3	064 2.3 1.1	017 0.8 0.5	047 0.9 0.4
-5	078 0.6 0.3	124 1.3 0.6	021 1.5 0.7	007 0.6 0.3	030 2.2 1.0	023 0.6 0.3		073 2.0 1.0	016 1.7 1.0	025 0.4 0.2
-4	154 0.6 0.3	165 1.7 0.8	023 2.3 1.0	326 0.6 0.3	028 2.8 1.3	279 0.3 0.1	200 0.4 0.2	076 1.2 0.6	017 2.1 1.3	290 0.3 0.1
-3	188 1.1 0.5	184 2.0 1.0	023 2.3 1.1	304 0.7 0.3	024 2.6 1.2	239 0.7 0.3	225 1.0 0.5	231 1.2 0.6	017 2.1 1.2	256 1.0 0.5
-2	204 1.4 0.7	205 1.8 0.9	029 1.9 0.9	283 0.7 0.3	024 1.8 0.8	235 1.0 0.5	231 1.2 0.6	228 1.0 0.5	019 1.7 1.0	247 1.3 0.6
-1	217 1.5 0.7	233 1.5 0.7	039 1.2 0.5	258 0.6 0.3	020 0.9 0.4	235 1.2 0.6	233 1.1 0.5	241 2.0 1.0	025 1.0 0.6	236 1.2 0.5
0	230 1.3 0.6	253 1.2 0.6	099 0.3 0.1	215 0.6 0.3	215 0.5 0.2	235 1.0 0.5	239 0.7 0.3	253 2.1 1.0	182 0.4 0.2	228 0.9 0.4
+1	249 0.9 0.4	295 0.9 0.4	200 1.3 0.6	179 0.7 0.3	208 1.8 0.8	235 1.0 0.5	237 0.2 0.1	254 1.6 0.8	194 1.4 0.8	218 0.6 0.3
+2	300 0.5 0.2	342 1.2 0.6	205 2.2 1.0	148 0.6 0.3	207 2.8 1.3	112 0.1 0.0	033 0.3 0.1	250 0.9 0.5	200 2.1 1.2	175 0.2 0.1
+3	001 0.8 0.4	001 1.7 0.8	206 2.6 1.2	123 0.6 0.3	210 2.8 1.3	068 0.6 0.3	034 0.9 0.4	241 0.1 0.1	201 2.3 1.4	093 0.5 0.2
+4	017 1.4 0.6	014 1.9 0.9	207 2.1 1.0	102 0.6 0.3	207 2.1 1.0	066 1.0 0.5	039 1.2 0.6	050 0.6 0.3	202 1.9 1.1	070 1.1 0.5
+5	030 1.7 0.8	030 1.6 0.8	208 1.3 0.8	079 0.5 0.3	194 1.1 0.5	046 1.1 0.5	046 1.0 0.5	052 1.3 0.6	198 1.0 0.6	057 1.3 0.6
+6	044 1.4 0.7	056 1.3 0.6	000 0.2 0.1	049 0.5 0.3	064 0.5 0.3	054 1.0 0.5	052 0.9 0.4	062 2.1 1.0	025 0.2 0.1	050 1.1 0.5

For additional information, see Admiralty Tidal Stream Atlas NP256.

Tidal stream atlases

Again, you will be told which standard port the tidal stream atlas has been referenced to and you will use the tide table for this port.

As with tidal diamonds, you find the time of HW that will affect you and the range of the tide. You draw out a tidal hour diagram to establish which hour of the tide you are sailing on and then instead of reading the information off you have to measure the set of the tide with your plotter.

The rate of the tide is written on the arrow. For some reason they quote the neap rate before the spring rate. I called the IMO and asked why tidal diamonds give the spring rate first and tidal stream atlases give the neap rate first and got the response: 'Well, just because'. So that will have to do.

If you have a spring range then you will need to be looking at the higher rate of the tide, a neap rate, the lower rate of the tide. Or compute.

What's the smallest interval you would work out a tidal effect for?

Probably 30 minutes. Anything less is getting very fiddly. And if you are not setting off exactly half an hour away from the centre of the tidal hour, then delay until you are.

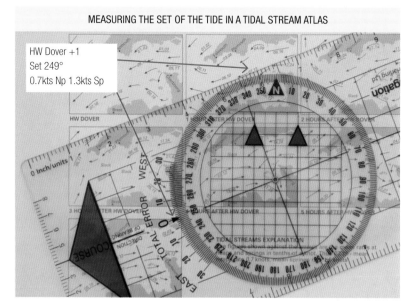

MEASURING THE SET OF THE TIDE IN A TIDAL STREAM ATLAS

HW Dover +1
Set 249°
0.7kts Np 1.3kts Sp

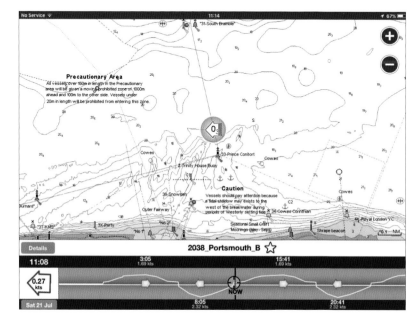

▲ Here you are sailing in HW+1. You measure the angle of the arrow to get the set, which is 249°T, and read off the rate, which is 0.7 knots at neaps and 1.3 knots at springs.

Checking what the tide app is telling us

Here (left) is Saturday, 21 July, off Cowes. It is 1108DST and the plotter shows the set as being roughly 275° and the rate 0.27 knots, which you would round to 0.3 knots.

You can check this.

HW Portsmouth was 0658DST 4.0m and LW 1.6m, range 2.4m.

Mean spring range Portsmouth is 3.9m and mean neap 1.9m, mid range 2.9m.

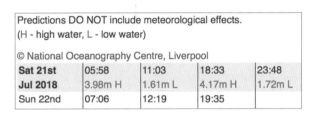

Predictions DO NOT include meteorological effects.
(H - high water, L - low water)

© National Oceanography Centre, Liverpool

Sat 21st	05:58	11:03	18:33	23:48
Jul 2018	3.98m H	1.61m L	4.17m H	1.72m L
Sun 22nd	07:06	12:19	19:35	

▼ *Portsmouth tidal curve and mean ranges.*   ▲ *Portsmouth tide times 21 July 2018.*

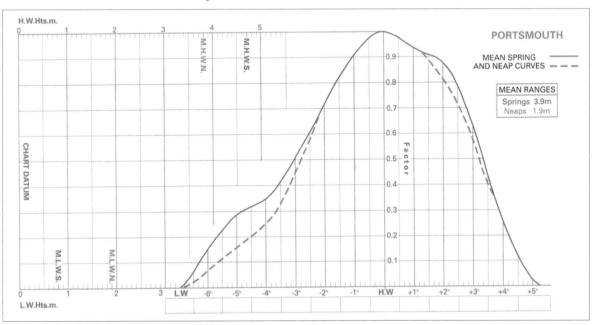

You are in the hour of HW+4.

SAT 21/7/18

HW PORTSMOUTH   0658 DST
              HW   4.0 m
              LW   1.6 m
              RANGE   2.4 m

0658 DST / 0628 HW
              0728
                +1
              0828
                +2
              0928
                +3
              1028
                +4
              1128

1108   HW + 4

Tidal diamond E on the chart tells you that the set and rate for the tide in this hour is 275° 0.5 knots springs and 0.2 knots neaps.

◇D 50°47'21 N 1 19·28W		◇E 50°46'53 N 1 17·59W		◇F 50°48'43 N 1 17·59W		◇G 50°47'03 N 1 16·79W	
58	1·1 0·5	084	2·5 1·2	022	1·8 0·9	076	1·2 0·6
56	1·0 0·5	090	2·7 1·3	038	1·0 0·5	085	1·5 0·8
55	1·1 0·5	091	2·7 1·4	070	0·4 0·2	085	1·7 0·9
50	1·3 0·6	090	2·2 1·1	058	0·4 0·2	088	1·6 0·8
43	0·7 0·3	096	0·9 0·4	019	1·4 0·7	082	1·5 0·8
23	0·8 0·4	259	0·7 0·3	008	0·5 0·2	093	0·6 0·3
31	2·1 1·0	267	2·8 1·4	232	1·0 0·5	255	0·6 0·3
36	1·8 0·9	268	3·8 1·9	230	1·1 0·5	268	2·0 1·0
31	1·7 0·8	269	3·0 1·5	226	1·2 0·6	268	2·3 1·1
30	1·4 0·6	266	1·8 0·8	205	1·4 0·7	263	1·8 0·9
26	0·9 0·4	275	0·5 0·2	180	2·4 1·2	230	0·8 0·4
	0·0 0·0	083	0·8 0·4	070	0·2 0·1	167	0·4 0·2
57	1·1 0·5	084	2·0 1·0	025	1·6 0·8	096	1·0 0·5
◇P 50°46'13 N 1 11·89W		◇Q 50°47'03 N 1 11·39W		◇R 50°45'13 N 1 09·49W		◇S 50°45'93 N 1 09·49W	
10	1·2 0·6	117	0·8 0·4	110	1·3 0·6	103	1·2 0·6
16	1·7 0·9	114	0·8 0·4	115	1·5 0·7	109	1·6 0·8
26	1·7 0·9	108	0·6 0·3	118	1·1 0·6	114	1·7 0·8
34	1·1 0·6	087	0·3 0·2	120	0·3 0·2	127	1·1 0·5

To establish the rate when you are neither at springs, nor neaps, nor exactly midway between, the easiest thing is to take the range of the tide you are dealing with and by dividing it by the mean range, establish the percentage and then apply this percentage to the spring rate of the tide.

Today's range is 2.4m. As a percentage of the mean spring range of 3.9m, this is 61%. Then 61% of the spring rate for the hour of 0.5 is 0.3 knots.

So a quick check tells you that the tidal streams program within the Navionics app is giving you the correct info.

Computation of tidal rates

A chart plotter gives you the set of the tide and rate of the tide 24/7. And it measures the range of the tide against the mean ranges to give you an exact rate of tide. You can do this manually as you have seen when the range matches up with springs, or neaps or midway, but what do you do when it doesn't?

The correct way to do it for an RYA Yachtmaster exam is to use the 'Computation of Tidal Rates' table.

This table is based on Dover. All tidal stream atlases in the UK will either be based on Dover or will give the differences in time to HW Dover.

You want to know the rate of tide in the north channel at the western end of the Solent by Hurst Castle.

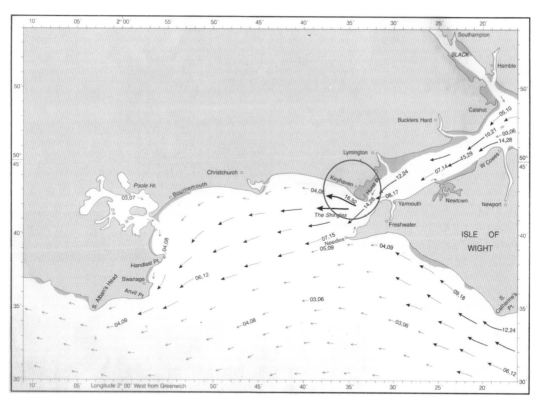

▲ HW hour Portsmouth, neap rate 1.6, spring rate 3.2.

It is 11 August, HW Portsmouth is 1202DST and you are sailing at 1227, so you are in the HW hour.

The range at Dover on the day is 6.1m (6.8m HW less 0.7m LW).

The rates are 1.6 and 3.2 knots.

Place the 1.6 on the neap line on the Computation of Tidal Rates table and the 3.2 on the spring line. Draw a line between the two points and beyond the 3.2 point as the range in Dover on the day is higher than the mean.

Find 6.1 on the left-hand side, the Dover ranges, come across to the spring/neap line and then up to read off 3.3 knots.

Your chart plotter says you will have 3 knots, a little less than you think.

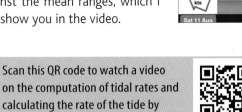

▶ *3 knots according to the chart plotter.*

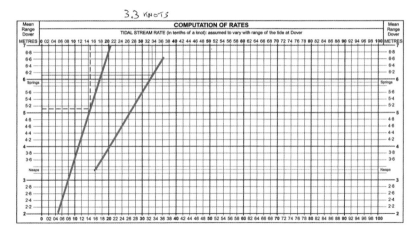

▲ *Computation of Tidal Rates table with drawing – 3.3 knots.*

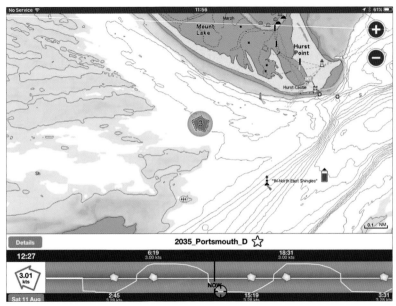

Another way of doing this is to take the percentage of the actual ranges of high and low water against the mean ranges, which I will show you in the video.

Scan this QR code to watch a video on the computation of tidal rates and calculating the rate of the tide by comparing the actual ranges of high and low water with the mean ranges.

9 Leeway

Leeway is the degree to which the wind blows you off course. Any boat that presents any superstructure or sails that the wind can blow against will experience leeway.

How much leeway you allow for when calculating your actual course over the ground depends on the type of boat. A long-keeled traditional sailing boat with very little of the boat above the water will experience far less leeway than one with a short fin keel and high topsides.

▶ *Pilot cutter – most of her is in the water.*

▼ *A modern yacht with high topsides and less of a keel.*

> **i Leeway ready reckoner**
>
> **Estimated position:**
> Wind on port – add leeway to course
> Wind on starboard – deduct leeway from course
>
> **Course to steer:**
> Wind on port – deduct it from course to steer
> Wind on starboard – add it to course to steer

Motorboats experience leeway, although generally they are going so fast – by comparison with sailing boats – that the degree to which they are pushed off course by the wind is a very small percentage of their total distance travelled.

▲ *About 5° of leeway.*

Leeway is a rough approximation.

Allow:
- 5° of leeway for winds up to Force 5
- 10° for winds above that.

You can see the amount of leeway you are experiencing by looking at the wake.

You take leeway into account at the beginning when working out your estimated position and at the end when working out a course to steer.

If the wind is on your port side the boat will be pushed positively round the compass and if the wind is on your starboard side the boat will be pushed negatively round the compass.

Estimated position

Establishing where you are is not something you need to worry about with chart plotters as they give you your position to within 2 metres, 24 hours a day, 365 days a year. That's the beauty of them. You always know where you are.

But if you are going to pass your exams – RYA Royal Yachting Association, ASA American Sailing Association, MCA Maritime & Coastguard Association, IYT International Yacht & Maritime Training – then you will need to be able to work out an estimated position (EP) on a paper chart.

Estimating your position is a reactive exercise. You start from a known position and sail on a course at a certain speed for a certain time so you must be, well, *here*. You make a mark on the chart where you think you are and this is your **dead reckoning (DR)** position – derived simply from the course you steered and the distance you travelled.

But the tide has been affecting you as you have travelled and it may have pushed you well off course, so you are actually nowhere near where your dead reckoning position says you are.

How to work out an estimated position

You start here. Mark your start position with a dot and a circle round it, the symbol for a fix, and the time beside it, say 0800, and the reading from the log, say 30 miles. You then sail on a course of 070°T for an hour at 6 knots, so you draw the bearing line on the chart at 070°, long enough for you to be able to mark off 6 miles. That is your DR position. But during that hour, a tide running at 135°T at a speed of 2.0 knots has been pushing you off course.

Draw in this tide line, also called a tidal vector, to your DR position – that is where you are. Mark your EP with a dot and a triangle around it and the time,

▶ *Garmin 192.*

▼ *Dead Reckoning (DR).*

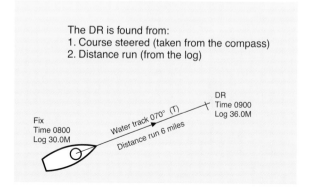

The DR is found from:
1. Course steered (taken from the compass)
2. Distance run (from the log)

Fix
Time 0800
Log 30.0M

Water track 070° (T)
Distance run 6 miles

DR
Time 0900
Log 36.0M

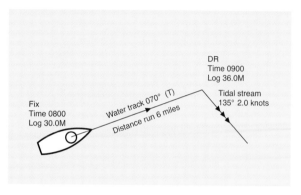

Fix
Time 0800
Log 30.0M

Water track 070° (T)
Distance run 6 miles

DR
Time 0900
Log 36.0M

Tidal stream
135° 2.0 knots

▲ *Estimated position (EP) 1.*

now 0900, and the log reading, now 36 miles. And then using your dividers, establish the latitude and longitude of this position.

Of course, while this allows for the effect of the tide, it does not allow for the effect of the wind – leeway. Leeway is the degree to which the wind has pushed you off course.

If you have wind on the port side, this will blow you off course positively around the compass. Add it to your heading. If you have wind on starboard, it will blow you off course negatively around the compass. Take it away from your heading.

Here you have 5° of leeway from wind on the port side. While your heading was 070°, your track through the water will be 075°. This is the bearing line that you'll draw on the chart before applying the effect of the tide.

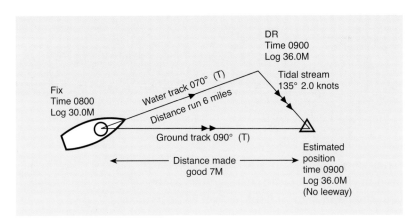

▲ *Estimated position (EP) 2.*

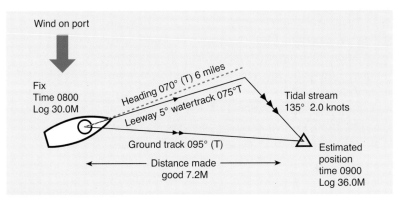

▲ *Estimated position (EP) 3, including leeway.*

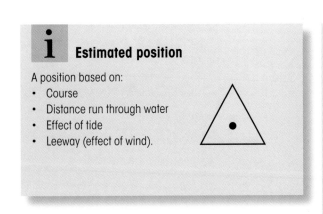

Estimated position

A position based on:
• Course
• Distance run through water
• Effect of tide
• Leeway (effect of wind).

▶ *Water track, ground track, tidal stream are vectors. A vector is just a line that has a length and a direction.*

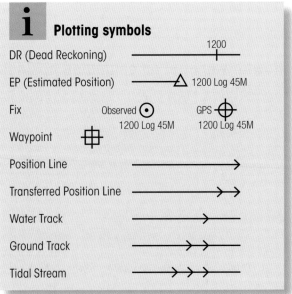

Plotting symbols

DR (Dead Reckoning)	
EP (Estimated Position)	
Fix	Observed / GPS
Waypoint	
Position Line	
Transferred Position Line	
Water Track	
Ground Track	
Tidal Stream	

EXAMPLE

It is Tuesday 15 May, and you are just outside Salcombe in position

50°12'.5N by 003°46'.0W.

It is 1321 and you sail on a compass course of 135°C at 6 knots – your log reads 42 miles at 1321 and 48 miles at 1421.

Your boat experiences 6°E deviation on that heading.

The chart tells you that magnetic variation is 1°W.

The wind is blowing F4 from the NE and you estimated your leeway to be 5°.

You will use tidal diamond B for the set and rate of the tide.

Where will you be at 1421?

Step 1 Plot your fix at 1321 50°12'.5N by 003°46'.0W on the chart. Write the time and the log reading 42M beside the fix.

Step 2 Establish your true course to plot on the chart.

135°C
+ 6°E Deviation
141°M
 - 1°W Variation
140°T
+ 5° Leeway – wind on port = + compass
145°T

5° Leeway on port should be added to the course. See page 73.
Give the line one arrow – this is your water track.

Step 3 Measure 6 miles on the latitude scale and mark 6 miles along your course line.
This is your DR position.

To find your EP, you need to allow for the effect of the tide.

Tidal diamonds on this chart are referenced to HW Plymouth.

Tidal Streams referred to HW at PLYMOUTH (DEVONPORT)

Hours	Geographical Position / Directions of streams (degrees)	Rates at spring tides (knots)	Rates at neap tides (knots)	A 50°07·84N 3 55·27W			B 50°10·04N 3 38·87W			C 50°12·54N 4 05·27W			D 50°13·04N 3 37·07W			E 50°17·04N 3 35·07W			F 50°18·04N 3 20·08W			G 50°18·3 4 07·7		
Before High Water 6				282	1·4	0·7	245	1·3	0·7	266	0·8	0·4	203	2·2	1·1	206	1·0	0·5	227	1·0	0·5	297	0·8	0
5				282	1·4	0·6	243	2·0	1·0	284	0·8	0·4	203	2·1	1·1	208	1·2	0·6	232	1·4	0·7	306	0·7	0
4				286	1·1	0·5	241	2·1	1·0	294	0·8	0·4	192	1·5	0·8	213	1·0	0·5	234	1·5	0·7	307	0·6	0
3				291	0·3	0·1	244	1·3	0·7	318	0·5	0·2	137	0·7	0·4	235	0·5	0·3	241	0·8	0·4	304	0·3	0
2				091	0·5	0·2	206	0·3	0·2	069	0·4	0·2	057	2·9	1·4	072	0·3	0·1	307	0·3	0·1	098	0·3	0
1				098	1·1	0·5	066	1·0	0·5	087	0·8	0·4	043	3·0	1·5	044	0·7	0·3	034	0·7	0·3	109	0·7	0
High Water				096	1·4	0·7	062	1·6	0·8	098	1·0	0·5	046	2·5	1·2	039	1·2	0·6	048	1·1	0·6	110	0·9	0
After High Water 1				103	1·3	0·6	059	2·0	1·0	110	0·9	0·4	049	2·2	1·1	031	1·1	0·5	055	1·4	0·7	111	0·8	0
2				105	0·9	0·4	053	1·8	0·9	129	0·6	0·4	061	1·4	0·7	035	0·8	0·4	061	1·4	0·7	121	0·6	0
3				129	0·2	0·1	060	1·0	0·5	170	0·2	0·1	137	0·7	0·4	044	0·5	0·2	060	0·8	0·4	156	0·3	0
4				261	0·4	0·2	100	0·3	0·2	267	0·2	0·1	186	1·5	0·8	046	0·1	0·1	074	0·3	0·2	265	0·4	0
5				273	0·9	0·4	226	0·5	0·3	271	0·6	0·3	200	2·1	1·0	214	0·5	0·2	201	0·2	0·1	294	0·7	0
6				277	1·3	0·6	248	1·1	0·5	264	0·8	0·4	202	2·2	1·1	209	0·8	0·4	222	0·8	0·4	296	0·8	0

	H 50°18·33N 4 10·87W			J 50°28·53N 3 22·58W		
-6	236	0·7	0·4	218	0·8	0·4
-5	264	0·6	0·3	226	0·9	0·5
-4	316	0·6	0·3	214	1·1	0·6
-3	031	0·5	0·2	211	0·6	0·3
-2	047	0·7	0·4	290	0·2	0·1
-1	053	1·0	0·5	011	0·4	0·2
	081	1·0	0·5	025	0·7	0·4
-1	111	0·8	0·4	036	0·7	0·4
-2	129	0·3	0·2	043	0·7	0·4
-3	235	0·3	0·1	060	0·5	0·3
-4	242	0·8	0·4	100	0·2	0·1

▲ Tidal diamonds on this chart referenced to HW Plymouth.

Continued ▶

Step 4 Find the time of HW Plymouth in the almanac for the tide you are sailing on: 1751UT. This needs one hour added to it to bring it into DST, so HW Plymouth is 1851. You are sailing on the flood tide.

▶ **Step 5** Find the range by taking the LW height from the HW height on this day. HW of 5.4m minus LW before of 0.7m = 4.7m, which according to the mean ranges on the tidal curve is springs.

▶ **Step 6** Establish which hour of the tide you are sailing in.

HW 1851 DST. HW hour 1821 to 1921. Sailing from 1321 to 1421 you are sailing in HW-5.

▼ **Step 7** Read off from the tidal diamond B the set and rate for 5 hours before HW, spring range and you get a set of 243°T and a rate of 2 knots.

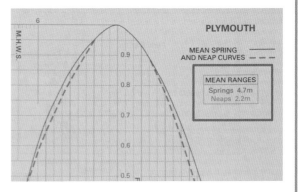

PLYMOUTH

MEAN SPRING ⎯⎯⎯
AND NEAP CURVES ⎯ ⎯ ⎯

MEAN RANGES
Springs 4.7m
Neaps 2.2m

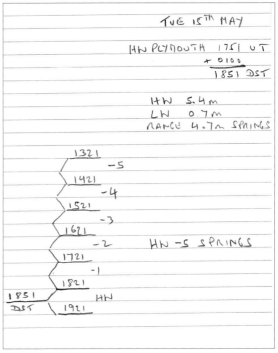

TUE 15ᵀᴴ MAY

HW PLYMOUTH 1751 UT
+ 0100
1851 DST

HW 5.4 m
LW 0.7 m
RANGE 4.7m SPRINGS

1321
        -5
1421
        -4
1521
        -3
1621
        -2   HW -5 SPRINGS
1721
        -1
1821
1851   HW
DST   1921

Tidal Streams referred to HW at |

il	A 50°07´·84N 3 55 ·27W		B 50°10´·04N 3 38 ·87W		C 50°12´·54N 4 05 ·27W	
282	1·4	0·7	245	1·3	0·7	266	0·8	0·4
282	1·4	0·6	243	2·0	1·0	284	0·8	0·4
286	1·1	0·5	241	2·1	1·0	294	0·8	0·4
291	0·3	0·1	244	1·3	0·7	318	0·5	0·2
091	0·5	0·2	206	0·3	0·2	069	0·4	0·2
098	1·1	0·5	066	1·0	0·5	087	0·8	0·4
096	1·4	0·7	062	1·6	0·8	098	1·0	0·5
103	1·3	0·6	059	2·0	1·0	110	0·9	0·4
105	0·9	0·4	053	1·8	0·9	129	0·6	0·4
129	0·2	0·1	060	1·0	0·5	170	0·2	0·1
261	0·4	0·2	100	0·3	0·2	267	0·2	0·1
273	0·9	0·4	226	0·5	0·3	271	0·6	0·3
277	1·3	0·6	248	1·1	0·5	264	0·8	0·4

Step 8 Apply this tide to the DR position – draw a line on the bearing of 243°T, give the line three arrows, it is your tide line. Mark off 2 miles along it.

Step 9 This then is your EP, which you mark with a dot with a triangle, the time beside it and the log reading, 48M. Finally, take the lat/long from the chart: 50°06'.75N by 003°43'.4W.

Step 10 The course line from your start position to your EP is your course over ground (COG) and if you measure the length of this and take it to the latitude scale it will give you your speed over ground (SOG).

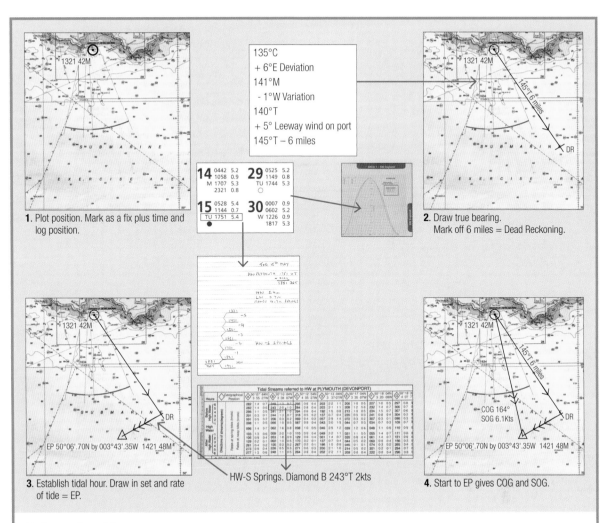

135°C
+ 6°E Deviation
141°M
- 1°W Variation
140°T
+ 5° Leeway wind on port
145°T – 6 miles

1. Plot position. Mark as a fix plus time and log position.

2. Draw true bearing. Mark off 6 miles = Dead Reckoning.

3. Establish tidal hour. Draw in set and rate of tide = EP.

HW–S Springs. Diamond B 243°T 2kts

4. Start to EP gives COG and SOG.

COG 164°
SOG 6.1Kts

EP 50°06'.70N by 003°43'.35W 1421 48M

Estimated position steps recap

The tide goes on at the end...

1. Plot position.
2. Draw in course.
3. Check which port tidal diamonds/tidal stream atlas referred to.
4. Go to the correct port and check HW for the day. HW – LW = range.
5. Work out the tidal hour.
6. Check mean ranges.
7. Check tidal diamond set and rate for the tidal hour.
8. Draw in tide.
9. Mark EP.
10. Start to EP gives COG and SOG.

Mark up your chartwork:

- One arrow – goes on your water track.
- Two arrows – go on your course over the ground. These are your two feet walking over the seabed.
- Three arrows – go on your tide line.

Scan this QR code to watch a video on estimated position.

The log and the logbook

The log is something that measures the distance we travel through the water, be it an impeller, Doppler effect or a pitot tube. Just like in a car, it has a trip meter and this you reset regularly.

The logbook is where you list your passages and every hour: the time, barometer reading, visibility, wind direction and strength, log reading, compass heading, latitude and longitude and any notes.

Overlapping tidal hours

Notice how the hour that you were sailing in during the example was exactly across a tidal hour? This is always the case for RYA Day Skipper level questions. In real life, if you had been a few minutes adrift from the tidal hour, say sailing at 1312 for a tidal hour that started at 1321, you'd still have used HW-5 hour. You'd only use half an hour of tide from one hour and half an hour from another hour, if you really were half an hour adrift from the tidal hour.

A PICTORIAL VIEW OF DEVIATION, MAGNETIC VARIATION AND LEEWAY

315° Compass to 293° true including leeway

Deviation 6° W
Magnetic variation 6° W
Leeway wind strbrd 10°

—— Compass course steered (heading)	315° C
—— Allowing for 6° W deviation	309° M
—— Allowing for 6° W magnetic variation	303° T
—— Allowing for 10° lee way wind on strbrd	293° (T)

▲ Here you have 6°W deviation, 6°W magnetic variation and 10° leeway from a wind on starboard. I have exaggerated the angles for effect.

135° Compass to 139° true including leeway

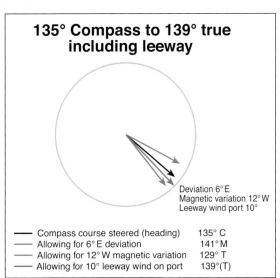

Deviation 6° E
Magnetic variation 12° W
Leeway wind port 10°

—— Compass course steered (heading)	135° C
—— Allowing for 6° E deviation	141° M
—— Allowing for 12° W magnetic variation	129° T
—— Allowing for 10° leeway wind on port	139° (T)

▲ Here you are in the USA with 6°E deviation, 12°W magnetic variation and 10° leeway from a wind on port. I have exaggerated the angles for effect.

Projected estimated position

You can also use the EP to project where you might be at a certain time.

Say you are in the Gulf of Saint-Malo, to the west of the Cherbourg Peninsula, approaching Port-Bail. The skipper has asked you to let him know when you'll arrive at the 5m contour as he is keen to tack before then.

To create a projected EP:

Establish your position by drawing a line on the raster chart of the electronic chart plotter from the boat to the centre of the compass rose. This tells you that it bears 152° 3.95 miles from the boat and can be plotted on the chart.

You don't get compass roses on vector (layered) charts, only on raster charts, which are a direct copy of the paper version and are not layered.

You're sailing on a course of 045°C on a broad reach on starboard, The wind is 10 knots from the south. You're not experiencing any leeway. There is no deviation on this course and magnetic variation on this chart is 0°. So your 045°C is also your true bearing and can be drawn on the chart.

You're doing 5 knots through the water. You will use tidal diamond R on this chart for the set and rate of the tide. The time is 0710 on Wednesday 10 March. The log at 0710 reads 125 miles.

Step 1 Draw the bearing of your course through the water on the chart and mark off 5 miles down it. This would be your DR position after one hour.

Step 2 Check the tidal diamonds to see which standard port they are referred to – St Helier.

Step 3 Establish which hour of the tide you are sailing in. HW St Helier is 1040UT. Sailing at 0710

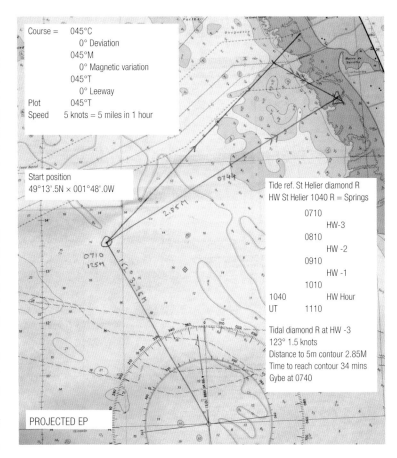

you are sailing during HW-3. The range (HW 10.8m – LW 1.2m) is 9.6m, which is springs.

Step 4 Tidal diamond R gives you a set and rate for HW-3 springs of 123°T 1.5 knots. Draw in the tide line, the tidal vector from your DR position. Mark off 1.5 miles. This is your EP.

Step 5 Draw a line from your EP to your start position. This is your COG.

Step 6 Measure the distance along the COG from your start position to the point you cross the 5m contour. This is 2.85M.

Step 7 2.85M ÷ 5M is 57%. 57% of 60 minutes is 34.2 minutes. You will cross the 5m contour at 0744. Advise the skipper to gybe on to port at 0740, to be safe.

On an electronic chart plotter you'd measure from your boat to the 5m contour and use the COG line for the bearing – this allows for the tide – and you could tell the skipper in an instant. You can also watch your progress towards the 5m contour on the chart plotter.

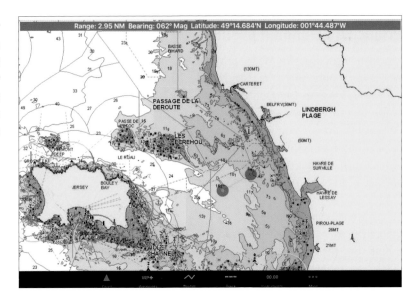

Range: 2.95 NM Bearing: 062° Mag Latitude: 49°14.684'N Longitude: 001°44.487'W

▶ *Instant projected EP on a plotter.*

i Preparing your course steered for drawing on the chart

Step 1 Your course will have come from your steering compass and this will be in °Compass and subject to some deviation. So you need to allow for deviation to get °C to °M.
Step 2 Allow for magnetic variation to get °M to °T.
Step 3 Allow for leeway.

Example
You're in Chesapeake Bay in the USA on a course of 270°C. Deviation on this heading is 4°E. Magnetic variation is 11°W and you have 5° of leeway from a northerly wind.

270°	Compass
+ 4°	Easterly deviation
274°	Magnetic
– 11°	Westerly magnetic variation
263°	True
– 5°	Leeway due to wind on starboard (wind from the north, your course of 270° means you are on a beam reach.
258°T	Bearing you will draw on the chart.

Advanced estimated position

Say you want to establish your estimated position and you have been sailing for two hours, over two tidal hours. Then, having established your DR position you'd add the first tidal vector and then the second tidal vector on to the end of the first and this would then give you your EP.

If you have had to alter course during the period, perhaps to avoid another vessel, you'd draw in your first course, then the course alteration and your second course and finally apply the two tidal vectors at the end.

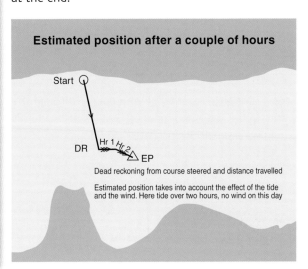

Estimated position after a couple of hours

Start

DR   Hr 1 Hr 2   △ EP

Dead reckoning from course steered and distance travelled

Estimated position takes into account the effect of the tide and the wind. Here tide over two hours, no wind on this day

EXAMPLE

Let's say you started from a position of 50°08'.6N by 045°46'.0W a couple of miles south of Dodman Point and sailed on a true course, net of leeway, of 045°T for 45 minutes and then had to alter course to starboard on to 075°T for 15 minutes to give way to a trawler. Then to compensate and try to get back on track you altered course to 015°T for 15 minutes, after which you resumed your original course of 045°T. You would draw these courses on the chart. You were doing an estimated 6 knots through the water.

Step 1 Draw in course 1, 045°T for 4.5 miles.

Step 2 Draw in course 2, 075°T for 1.5 miles.

Step 3 Draw in course 3, 015°T for 1.5 miles.

Step 4 Draw in course 4, 045°T for 4.5 miles.

This is your DR position.

Step 5 Apply the set and rate for the tide for the first hour. You get this from tidal diamond E on the chart: 195°T 0.9 knots.

Step 6 On the end of this, apply the set and rate for the tide for the second hour. This, from tidal diamond G on the chart, is 263°T 1.5 knots.

This is your EP.

Mark it with a dot with a triangle round it, the time and the log reading.

In a real example, the courses would be in °C and need converting to °M and then to °T and there would be leeway to allow for. Then you would need to work out which two hours of the tide you were sailing on, the range of the tide for the day, if you were on springs or neaps or somewhere in between and the rate of the tide for each hour. The set would be what you were given in the tidal diamond table or the tidal stream atlas.

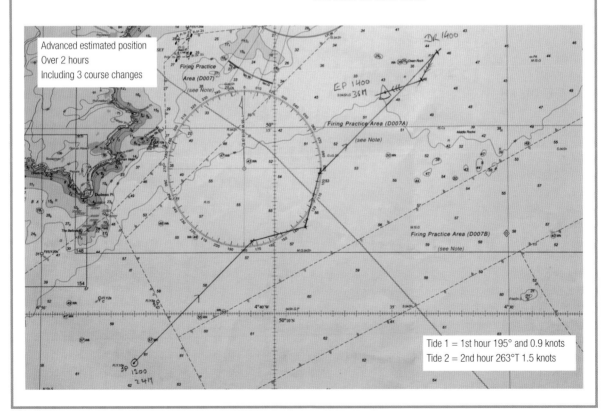

Advanced estimated position
Over 2 hours
Including 3 course changes

Tide 1 = 1st hour 195° and 0.9 knots
Tide 2 = 2nd hour 263°T 1.5 knots

Running fix

Using one charted object

Now you have mastered the art of working with the tidal vector (the tide line), I can show you my favourite navigational technique. It's called the running fix.

If all the electrics have died, your tablet is giving you the yellow warning triangle because it has overheated and you've lost signal on your phone, then you can still find out where you are, as long as you can see just one charted mark. Here you have a monument on the headland (1).

Take the bearing of the monument, note down the time, your heading and the log reading (2).

Navigators of old would always take a bearing when they spotted a prominent charted mark and, with the time, heading and log reading, would put it in their pocket. They never knew when they might need it.

Allow for magnetic variation and plot the bearing on the chart. At this time you must be down this line somewhere, only you are not quite sure where.

▲ *Conspicuous obelisk on Inner Froward Point, Dartmouth.*

Make a note of the course you are steering and the log reading.

An hour later, take another bearing on the monument and plot it on the chart. Now you must be down this line somewhere, but again you are not quite sure where (3).

If you now apply your heading in °T to any point on the first bearing line and mark off the distance you have travelled in the hour, this will give you a notional DR position (4).

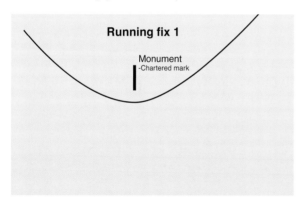

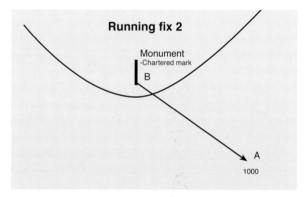

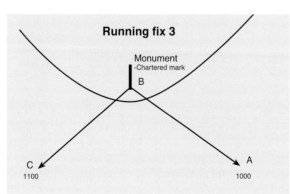

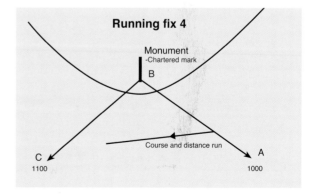

Then allow for the tide at the DR point (5). If you work parallel to your first bearing line and transfer it over, where it cuts your second bearing line, having gone through the end of your tidal vector, is your position (6).

It doesn't matter where you start from along the first bearing line. I have had a class of 20 students do this and naturally they all started in different places along the first bearing line and they all came to exactly the same position on the second bearing line.

For me, the running fix is as good a position fix as you can get and, of course, you can back it up with a depth. And if you are going to go further with navigation, perhaps to RYA Oceanmaster and astro navigation, you have just been introduced to the transferred position line.

If the charted mark will only be in sight for a short while, say half an hour, then do a half-hour plot. Plot the distance you will have run in 30 minutes and use half the rate of the tide.

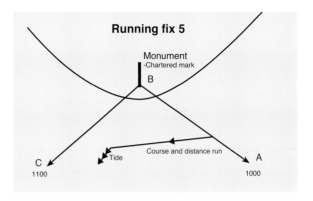

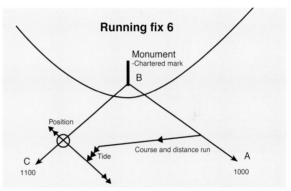

EXAMPLE

You are just off Cape Otway in SE Australia. You can see the lighthouse. You take a bearing on it at 0900 – 40°T – and then again at 1000 – 315°T. Mark off your course, 090°T at 6 knots, starting anywhere along your A–B line. Allow a tide according to the information on the chart of 1 knot setting in the direction of 140°T. Transfer the 0900 position line and where it cuts the C–B line, having gone through the end of the tidal vector, is where you are.

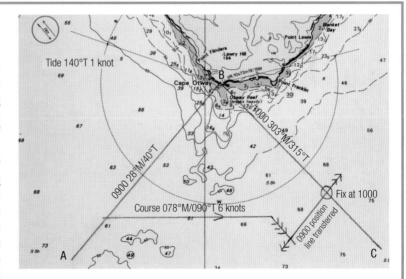

▲ *Magnetic variation in this part of the world, according to the Admiralty Chart, was 11°45'E in 1999, moving 1'E every year since. In 2018 it was 12°4'E, rounded to 12°E. So for the bearing of 40°T at 0900 your magnetic compass would have read 28°M and for the 1000 bearing of 315°T it would have read 303°M.*

Using two charted objects

You can also find your position by running fix using two separate marks and carrying a position line forward. Eric Hiscock did this when coming up the Channel one mouldy night. At 2315 he was able to get the bearing of the light on Portland Bill – 332°M – so he was somewhere down this line. He noted the log reading and set a course for the Needles, 068°M. By 0200 and having done 16 miles, he could no longer see the light on Portland Bill as it was shrouded in fog, but he could see the light on Anvil Point and he took the bearing – 40°M. He converted his bearings into °T and marked them on the chart. He then allowed for the tide and, transferring the position line at 2315, where it cut his position line at 0200, having gone through the end of the tidal vector, was where he was. Rather closer in to Anvil Head than he had thought, so he set a new course for the Needles – 076°M.

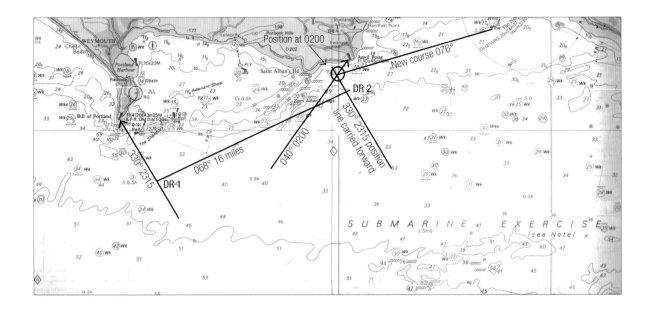

 Scan this QR code to watch a video on the running fix.

11

What if the GPS dies?

You have a compass, but you have no GPS, no radar, no radio, no chart plotter and all the phones are out of battery, so now where are you?

The smart money will have been keeping a paper plot as back-up. In that case, you will only be at most an hour from your last position. That's the stress-free way of doing things. Just saying.

But even if you didn't keep a paper plot, all is not lost.

If you can identify land and you have a compass and a chart, you can take a fix.

If you can't see land, you know where you started from and roughly how fast you've been going and on what course, so you can do a couple of things:

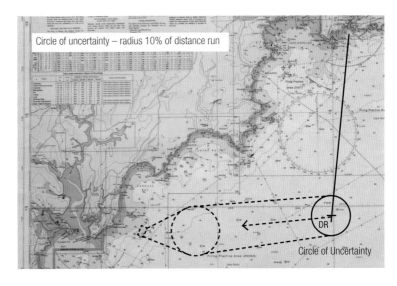

Circle of uncertainty – radius 10% of distance run

Circle of Uncertainty

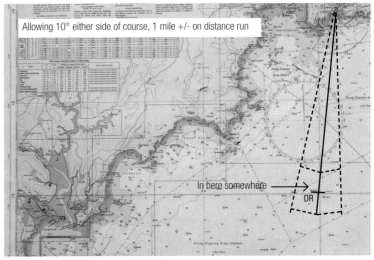

Allowing 10° either side of course, 1 mile +/- on distance run

In here somewhere

1. Draw a 'Circle of Uncertainty'.

Take 10% of the distance travelled as the radius of the circle and draw a circle at your 'Dead Reckoning' position.

Now sail your Circle of Uncertainty, which will increase in size, until you can reduce it, say, by crossing a depth contour.

2. Create a 'Box of Inexactitude'.

Estimate your course and allow 10° either side of it. Estimate your speed and allow 1 knot either side of this. This is your Box of Inexactitude, you're in here somewhere.

It's unnerving to be in an area rather than to be given your position to within a couple of metres, but as long as there is nothing you can hit, you'll be fine.

If you have been plonked in the sea by some magic hand and have no idea where you started from or where you are, there will be some clues to help you.

Where's the sun?

If you have a watch with traditional hands:

- Northern hemisphere – point the hour hand at the sun and bisect the angle between this and 12. That will be south.
- Southern hemisphere – point the 12 o'clock position at the sun and bisect the angle between this and the hour hand and that will be north.

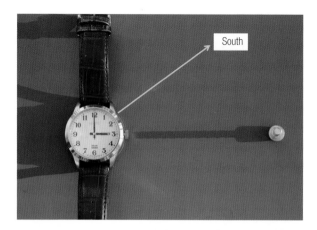

The sun also rises in the east and sets in the west.

If you head east or west you should find land. Unless, of course, you are sailing in the latitude of 57°S, which is just far enough from Cape Horn not to see it and, because there is nothing to hit down there, you'd just keep going round and round the world. Still, it would be very cold and unpleasant. And you'd probably get the idea that this exercise was going nowhere.

Night time?

a. In the northern hemisphere, you'll be able to see the Pole Star. Use the Great Bear to find this. Take the Plough – the last two stars on the pan (Merak and Dubhe) point to the North Star, Polaris, the Pole Star.

b. In the southern hemisphere, use the Southern Cross to find south. Take a line from the top of the cross to the bottom and extend it 4.5 times beyond this. A line to the horizon at this points gives you due south. You can check this by taking a line from between the two pointer stars: where this meets the imaginary line from the cross is the point to drop a line to the horizon to mark south.

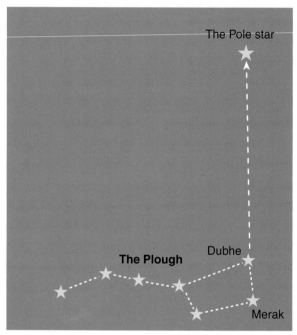

▲ *How to find the Pole Star.*

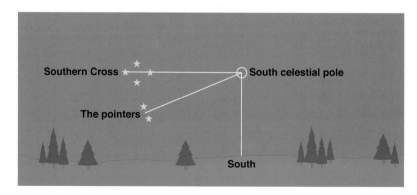

▶ *How to find south using the Southern Cross.*

c. Orion is very handy because Mintaka, the western-most star in its belt, rises in the east and sets in the west.

According to what I read, Orion is clearly visible in the night sky from November to February in either the northern or southern hemisphere. I am at 51°36'N and I have been viewing Orion since 30 August in the early hours of the morning. I know because I have been trying to get a good photo of it in different lights. And according to my Stellarium program I will lose it again at the end of April. So I see Orion not just from November to February but from late August to April.

d. Finally, you can always tell how far you are from shore when you see a charted light. Observe the point at which the light breaks the horizon or dips down below it, check your height of eye and then consult the Dipping Distance table in the almanac. With a bearing on the light, you have its direction and the line you are on and now you have your distance off, so you have a reasonable indication of where you are. You do need to have an almanac on board to be able to do this, of course.

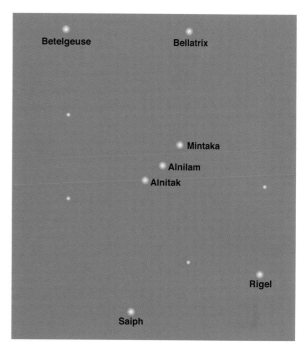

▲ *Orion.* ▼ *Mintaka rising in the east.*

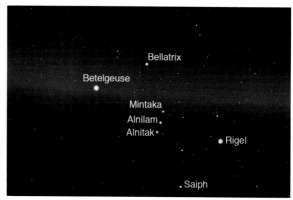

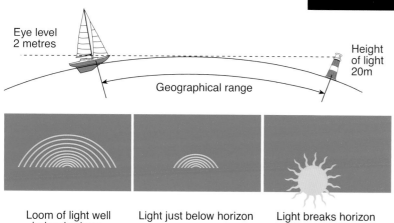

Eye level 2 metres

Height of light 20m

Geographical range

Loom of light well below horizon

Light just below horizon

Light breaks horizon (Rising distance)

◀ *Fix by dipping or rising light.*

TABLE 2 (2)   Lights – distance off when rising or dipping (M)

Height of light		metres	1	2	3	4	Height of eye 5	6	7	8	9	10
metres	feet	feet	3	7	10	13	16	20	23	26	30	33
10	33		8·7	9·5	10·2	10·8	11·3	11·7	12·1	12·5	12·8	13·2
12	39		9·3	10·1	10·8	11·4	11·9	12·3	12·7	13·1	13·4	13·8
14	46		9·9	10·7	11·4	12·0	12·5	12·9	13·3	13·7	14·0	14·4
16	53		10·4	11·2	11·9	12·5	13·0	13·4	13·8	14·2	14·5	14·9
18	59		10·9	11·7	12·4	13·0	13·5	13·9	14·3	14·7	15·0	15·4
20	66		11·4	12·2	12·9	13·5	14·0	14·4	14·8	15·2	15·5	15·9
22	72		11·9	12·7	13·4	14·0	14·5	14·9	15·3	15·7	16·0	16·4
24	79		12·3	13·1	13·8	14·4	14·9	15·3	15·7	16·1	16·4	17·0
26	85		12·7	13·5	14·2	14·8	15·3	15·7	16·1	16·5	16·8	17·2
28	92		13·1	13·9	14·6	15·2	15·7	16·1	16·5	16·9	17·2	17·6
30	98		13·5	14·3	15·0	15·6	16·1	16·5	16·9	17·3	17·6	18·0
32	105		13·9	14·7	15·4	16·0	16·5	16·9	17·3	17·7	18·0	18·4
34	112		14·2	15·0	15·7	16·3	16·8	17·2	17·6	18·0	18·3	18·7
36	118		14·6	15·4	16·1	16·7	17·2	17·6	18·0	18·4	18·7	19·1
38	125		14·9	15·7	16·4	17·0	17·5	17·9	18·3	18·7	19·0	19·4
40	131		15·3	16·1	16·8	17·4	17·9	18·3	18·7	19·1	19·4	19·8
42	138		15·6	16·4	17·1	17·7	18·2	18·6	19·0	19·4	19·7	20·1
44	144		15·9	16·7	17·4	18·0	18·5	18·9	19·3	19·7	20·0	20·4
46	151		16·2	17·0	17·7	18·3	18·8	19·2	19·6	20·0	20·3	20·7
48	157		16·5	17·3	18·0	18·6	19·1	19·5	19·9	20·3	20·6	21·0
50	164		16·8	17·6	18·3	18·9	19·4	19·8	20·2	20·6	20·9	21·3
55	180		17·5	18·3	19·0	19·6	20·1	20·5	20·9	21·3	21·6	22·0
60	197		18·2	19·0	19·7	20·3	20·8	21·2	21·6	22·0	22·3	22·7
65	213		18·9	19·7	20·4	21·0	21·5	21·9	22·3	22·7	23·0	23·4
70	230		19·5	20·3	21·0	21·6	22·1	22·5	22·9	23·2	23·6	24·0
75	246		20·1	20·9	21·6	22·2	22·7	23·1	23·5	23·9	24·2	24·6
80	262		20·7	21·5	22·2	22·8	23·3	23·7	24·1	24·5	24·8	25·2
85	279		21·3	22·1	22·8	23·4	23·9	24·3	24·7	25·1	25·4	25·8
90	295		21·8	22·6	23·3	23·9	24·4	24·8	25·2	25·6	25·9	26·3
95	312		22·4	23·2	23·9	24·5	25·0	25·4	25·8	26·2	26·5	26·9
metres	feet	metres	1	2	3	4	5	6	7	8	9	10
Height of light		feet	3	7	10	13	16	20	23	26	30	33
							Height of eye					

▲ *Dipping Distance table from* Reeds Almanac.

12 Course to steer

Where estimated position is a reactive exercise, course to steer (CTS) is a proactive exercise. You determine the course you need to steer from the outset to get from your start position to your destination.

As you have discovered from EP, the tide and the wind will conspire to push you off course. So to be able to sail down a line from your start point to your destination you'll need to counter their effect. You'll need to create a course to steer to stay on that line.

Many chart plotters will calculate a course to steer for you.

But you must be able to work it out for yourself.

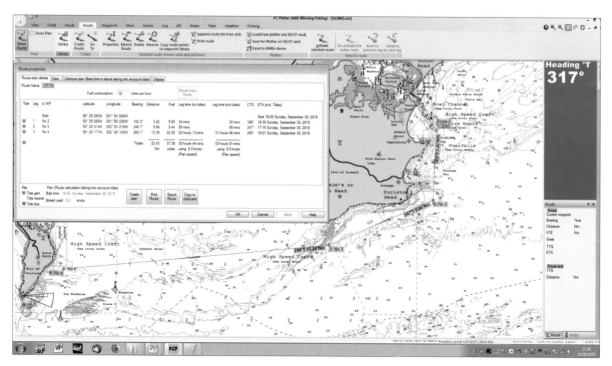

▲ Here, PC Plotter has given a course to steer, allowing for the tide, for each leg of a route from Poole to Portland Bill.

Because course to steer is proactive, allow for the effect of the tide at the beginning of the exercise.

You have a start position (A) and your destination (B).

Step 1 Draw a line from A to and through B.

Step 2 Measure the distance from A to B. If the distance matches the speed that you think you might sail at, then you will get there in roughly an hour and therefore will allow for one hour's worth of tidal effect. If it would take you two hours to get there, allow for two hours' worth; half an hour, then just half an hour of tidal effect, and so on.

Step 3 Having checked which port the tidal diamonds or tidal streams are referred to, go to the relevant tide table in the almanac.

Find the HW time for the tide you'll be sailing on and the heights of HW and LW. Establish which tidal hour you'll be sailing in and whether the tidal range is springs or neaps or somewhere in between.

Go to the tidal diamond and read off the direction in which the tide is setting and the rate in knots. If using a tidal stream atlas, measure the bearing of the tide with your plotter. And draw in the tide line, the tidal vector. Mark the end C.

Step 4 Set the dividers to the anticipated boat speed, measured off on the latitude scale. And then mark this distance off from C. Where it cuts the A–B line we will call D and the bearing of this line is your course to steer.

This is the course you need to steer in °T to counter the effect of the tide and allow you to sail along the A–B line – albeit crabbing somewhat.

We then need to convert this, the °T bearing of this course to steer, into °M, then to allow for leeway and then deviation to give the helmsman a compass course to steer.

How long will it take?

The distance A–B ÷ the distance A–D × the period = time in minutes.

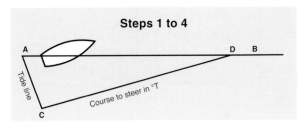
Steps 1 to 4

Example:
A–B = 6 miles, A–D = 5 miles, period = 1 hour:
$6 ÷ 5 = 1.2 × 60 = 72$ mins = 1 hr and 12 mins

 Handy reminder

- When working out an EP, apply the tide at the end.
- When working out a CTS, apply the tide at the start.

 Top tip – Drawing the CTS diagram to the side and scaling down

With CTS you don't need to do the diagram actually where you are on the chart, you can do it somewhere else and keep the area clear. Or indeed if you are working on a large-scale chart and the diagram will take up a lot of space on the chart then scale it down. As long as you use the same scale of units for distance, boat speed and rate of the tide, your diagram will be in proportion and you will arrive at the correct course to steer to allow for the effect of the tide.

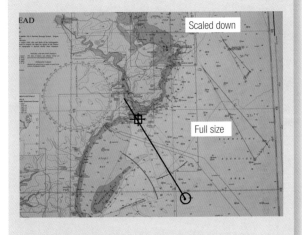

Remember that while you will work out a CTS to the last degree in the classroom, there is always something of an 'ish' factor when it comes to sailing the real thing. Will the leeway really be 5°? Will you sail a constant speed? Will you be able to sail the course to steer or will the wind head you? Huge accuracy in terms of establishing a course to steer, while important in exams, is hard to achieve in reality.

EXAMPLE

You have travelled from Cherbourg in France overnight and are heading for Poole.

It is 1043 on 16 May and the GPS indicates you are in position 50°35'.8N by 001°49'.5W. Plotting a position on a chart is quicker if you use a bearing and distance to a known mark than if you lay on the latitude and longitude, so you measured the bearing and distance from the boat to Anvil Point, which was 267°T 5.2.

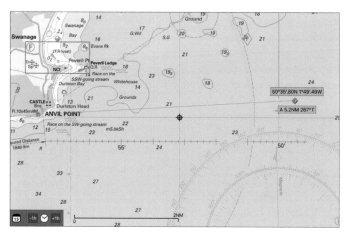

▲ Distance and bearing to Anvil Point lighthouse on Imray Navigator.

▲ Poole Bar Buoy – Imray.

▲ Anvil Point Lighthouse.

Step 1 Plot the start position on the chart and mark it with a dot with a circle round it and a cross through it to denote that it is a GPS fix. Write the time 1043 beside it and your log reading, which is 65 miles. This is A.

You have placed a waypoint near the Poole Bar Buoy starboard hand mark in position 50°39'.3N by 001°55'.1W.

Step 2 Plot the waypoint on the chart and mark it with a square and a cross through it. This is B.

Step 3 Draw a line from your position A to and through your waypoint B and measure the distance from A to B. It is 5 miles.

You sail at 6 knots so it will take you 1 hour.

Now you need to work out what the tide will do to you during this hour between 1043 and 1143.

You are going to use the tidal diamonds on this 'Bill of Portland to the Needles' chart. The tidal diamond that will affect you is Q and the chart tells you that the tidal diamonds are referred to HW Plymouth, so that is the tide table you will use.

Step 4 From the Plymouth tide table, find the HW time for 16 May:

16 May HW 0613UT	5.4m
Low water before was	0.6m
Range	4.8m

Plymouth tidal curve tells you this is springs.

If HW is 0613UT it will be 0713 in local time, which is DST, since you are in the month of May. You need to do a tidal hour diagram to work out what hour of the tide you will be sailing on at 1043 to 1143. You are sailing during the HW+4.

Step 5 Find the set and rate for tidal diamond Q for HW+4.

Set	046°T
Rate	1.3 knots at springs

Step 6 Dial 046°T into the plotter, place your pencil in the start position A, line up the central grid of the plotter with a horizontal or vertical line on the chart and draw in the tidal vector. Then with the dividers measure off from the latitude scale beside where you are working, 1.3 miles.

Now with one end of the dividers in A, mark off down the tide line 1.3 miles. This is point C.

Step 7 To establish the course to steer, set the dividers, on the latitude scale beside where you are working, to 6 miles. That is the distance you will travel through the water in one hour. With one end of the dividers in C, the end of the tide line, place the other end on the line A to B. And hold the dividers there while you bring the plotter up to them. It is much easier to get the bearing of this line accurately if you can slide the plotter up and down against the dividers.

Make sure the big arrow on the plotter is facing the direction of travel – your destination, the waypoint.

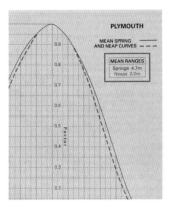

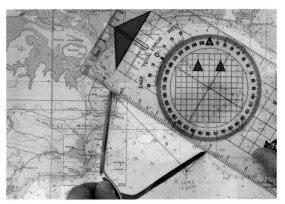

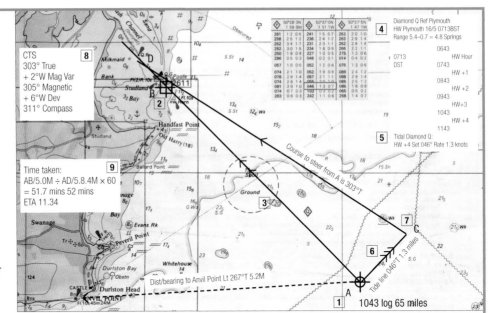

CTS [8]
303° True
+ 2°W Mag Var
305° Magnetic
+ 6°W Dev
311° Compass

Time taken: [9]
AB/5.0M ÷ AD/5.8.4M × 60
= 51.7 mins 52 mins
ETA 11.34

Course to steer from A is 303°T

Tidal Diamond Q: [5]
HW +4 Set 046° Rate 1.3 knots

Tide line 046°T 1.3 miles [6] [7]

Dist/bearing to Anvil Point Lt 267°T 5.2M

[1] 1043 log 65 miles

Diamond Q Ref Plymouth
HW Plymouth 16/5 0713BST
Range 5.4–0.7 = 4.8 Springs

0643
0713   HW Hour
DST   0743
        HW +1
        0843
        HW +2
        0943
        HW+3
        1043
        HW +4
        1143

▶ *From position A to waypoint off Poole – step by step guide.*

And with the central grid of the compass on the plotter lined up with a horizontal or vertical on the chart and the three arrows on the compass grid lined up with north, remove the dividers and draw in the course to steer bearing line. Then read off from the plotter the bearing of the course to steer – 303°T. This is the course you will steer from your start position A to sail down the line to your destination B. Mark the point where the distance travelled in one hour from C cuts the A to B line with a D.

Step 8 You need to convert this true bearing into a bearing that the helmsman can steer by.

303° True
+ 2°W magnetic variation – true to magnetic: west is best
305° Magnetic
+ 6°W Deviation – it's midway between 5° and 5°W according to the deviation curve so allow 6°W
311° Compass

Ask the helm to steer between 305° and 315°.

And if you steer this course from your start position A, you will travel down the bearing line to your waypoint B, albeit crabbing all the way.

Step 9 To establish how long it will take you to get there, measure the distance A to D, which is 5.8 miles.

Using the formula AB/AD × 60 = time taken, you have:

AB/5 miles ÷ AD/5.8 miles × 60 = 51.7 mins

You will arrive at the waypoint at 1043 + approximately 52 mins = 1135

Step 10 Mark up your chartwork:

1 arrow – Water track

2 arrows – Ground track

3 arrows – Tide

You can work this out well in advance of actually sailing. What you can't work out until you are there is what the wind will be doing and what leeway to allow. So on the day, you estimate the leeway. And in order to counter the effect of the wind, if the wind is on port, take leeway off the CTS and if it is on starboard add the leeway to it. Allow for leeway before establishing your deviation.

Of course, if you had been using your chart plotter you could have put in the waypoint and the plotter would have monitored your progress. This would not have given you a course to steer but would have shown you how much to correct your course as you approached the waypoint. In a strong cross tide, this could mean that as you neared the waypoint you could be pointing almost directly into the tide.

As we have seen, some plotters will actually give you a proper course to steer, allowing for the effect of the tide.

PC Plotter, for example, will tell you the best time to make the passage, allowing for the tides and the course you will need to steer. Programs like this can accept filters such as the maximum wave height you

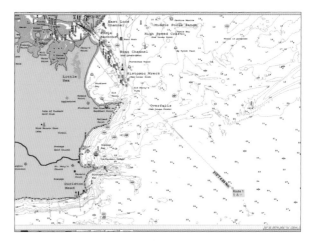

▲ *PC Plotter: entry to Poole.*

would like for the passage or the maximum wind speed and they will plan accordingly as they integrate data from a number of sources. Expedition, Adrena go even further, to tell you which sails to set, assuming you have inputted the polar data – that is, the wind speed, wind angle and boat speed data for each sail.

And once you select a time it will give you a CTS in °T for the passage.

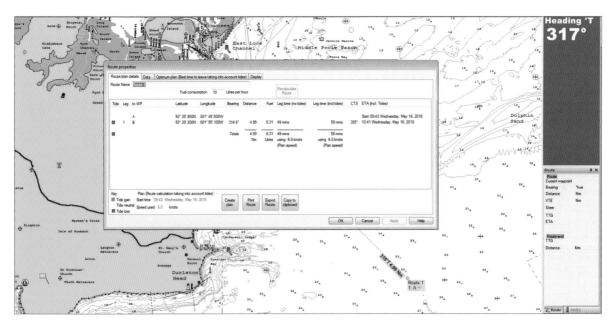

▲ *PC Plotter says the CTS is 305°T. This is because PC Plotter is cleverer than we are. We used one consistent hour of tidal set and rate. PC Plotter, knowing that the tide slackens during this hour, is reducing the effect of the tide across the hour and so we do not need so much of a course correction.*

PASSAGE LONGER THAN ONE HOUR?

If it will take longer than an hour to reach your destination then you need to allow for the effect of the relevant hours of the tide during which you will be sailing. Assuming there are no navigational hazards and it doesn't matter if you deviate from the rhumb line (the straight line from your start point to your destination), then you can apply all the tides, one after the other, from your start position.

When the tide runs more or less east for a few hours and then more or less west for a few hours, as it does in the English Channel, you can net off the effect of the tide.

If you assume that you will sail at a speed of 5 knots as you cross the 60 miles from the Needles to Cap de la Hague, it will take you 12 hours. This will be across two tides. On 25 July, this is an ebb tide from 0300 to 0900 and then a flood tide from 1000 to 1500, with an hour of slack tide in between. Netting off the two tides there is no effect either way, so you might as well sail straight towards your destination B on a dead-reckoning basis. The tide will sweep you in an 'S' but as there is nothing to hit, that will be fine. You will need to keep a sharp eye out for other shipping and remember that in the northern part of the channel the shipping is heading westward and in

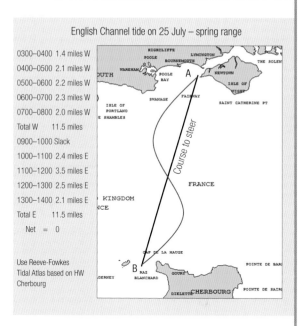

English Channel tide on 25 July – spring range

0300–0400	1.4 miles W
0400–0500	2.1 miles W
0500–0600	2.2 miles W
0600–0700	2.3 miles W
0700–0800	2.0 miles W
Total W	11.5 miles
0900–1000	Slack
1000–1100	2.4 miles E
1100–1200	3.5 miles E
1200–1300	2.5 miles E
1300–1400	2.1 miles E
Total E	11.5 miles
Net =	0

Use Reeve-Fowkes Tidal Atlas based on HW Cherbourg

▲ *Netting off the effect of the tide – 12 hours.*

the south, eastward. Ferries, of course, are dotting all over the place, as too are fishing boats.

Where it is important to stick to the rhumb line, you need to work out the CTS for every hour. Doing this you will travel further than if you allow the tide to drift you one way and the other.

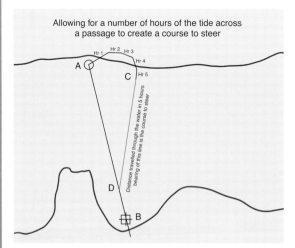

▲ *Allowing for a number of different tidal sets on a passage.*

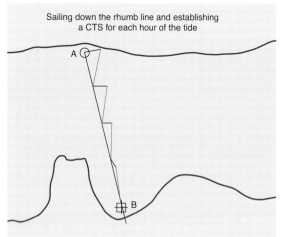

▲ *Sailing down the rhumb line, allowing for the tide each hour.*

Course To Steer in your head

Taking the example above when entering Poole, the bearing from your start position to the waypoint near Poole Bar Buoy is 315°T. The tide is running in the direction of 046°T at 1.3 knots, directly on your beam.

You can employ the 1 in 60 rule and use the formula:

60 × the speed of the tide ÷ boat speed
= the course correction required.
So 60 × 1.3 = 78 ÷ 6 knots = 13°.

You need to alter course by 13°, aiming into the tide.

The direct course, 315°T, less 13° gives a course to steer of 302°T – virtually the same as what you worked out in your CTS diagram on the chart and this time you did it in your head.

If the tide is not exactly on the beam, simply apply a percentage of the course correction.

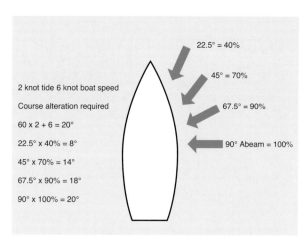

2 knot tide 6 knot boat speed

Course alteration required

60 x 2 + 6 = 20°

22.5° x 40% = 8°

45° x 70% = 14°

67.5° x 90% = 18°

90° x 100% = 20°

22.5° = 40%

45° = 70%

67.5° = 90%

90° Abeam = 100%

▲ *CTS in your head – allowance for course correction.*

Mind you, don't try doing CTS in your head during an exam. You might impress the examiner with your skill, but you will get no marks unless they can see some chartwork and nicely marked up, too. Water track one arrow, ground track two arrows, tide line three arrows.

i Cross track error (XTE)

Your electronic chart plotter will show you if you are off track. You can also set it to sound an alarm when you are a certain distance off course.

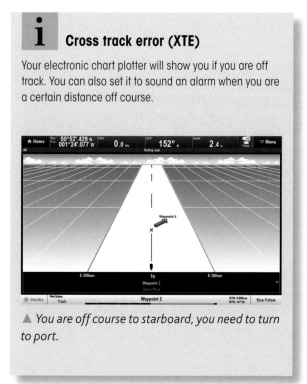

▲ *You are off course to starboard, you need to turn to port.*

Scan this QR code to watch a video on the practical application of course to steer.

13 Time zones

All time throughout the world is based on Greenwich Mean Time (GMT).

Greenwich is 'zero', from where time is measured.

As the world spins in an easterly direction, the sun rises for countries to the east of Greenwich ahead of us in the UK so they set their clocks earlier.

Countries to the west of Greenwich get their daylight later than Greenwich and set their clocks later than Greenwich.

There are 40 different world time zones.

Time zones that are ahead of GMT are referred to as 'minus' time zones.

Time zones behind GMT are known as 'plus' time zones.

This is slightly counter-intuitive until you remember that during the British Empire years, all orders would be given to the fleet around the world from the Admiralty in London and if you were sailing in the east you would have to take time off your local time to get back to London time. If you were in the west you would have to add time to your local time to get to London time.

 International Date Line

Time zones east of Greenwich are ahead until you get to the International Date Line at 180°E and 12 hours ahead, which meets with 180°W and 12 hours behind.

So crossing the International Date Line from west to east you gain a day.

Just west of the line is 1200 on Wednesday and just east of the line is 1200 on Tuesday so you get to have those 24 hours all over again.

And crossing from east to west you lose a day. Just east of the line is 1200 on Tuesday and just west of the line is 1200 on Wednesday so you have lost those 24 hours.

▲ *The Greenwich Meridian, 'zero', from where time and longitude are measured.*

Time is important when it comes to referring to tide tables. You need to know what they are telling you.

Tide tables in almanacs will be in the standard time of the country. For us that is GMT, also called Co-ordinated Universal Time (UTC), Universal Time (UT) or Zulu if you are in the forces, and you have to add one hour to those times that fall into the months of Daylight Saving Time (DST).

FALMOUTH LAT 50°09'N LONG 5°03'W
TIMES AND HEIGHTS OF HIGH AND LOW WATERS

STANDARD TIME (UT)
For Summer Time add ONE hour in non-shaded areas

Dates in red are SPRINGS
Dates in blue are NEAPS

YEAR 2016

SEPTEMBER		OCTOBER		NOVEMBER		DECEMBER	
Time m	Time m	Time m	Time m	Time m	Time m	Time m	Time m
1 0502 5.0 / 1151 0.5 / TH 1717 5.2 ●	**16** 0431 5.1 / 1111 0.6 / F 1648 5.4 / ○ 2335 0.4	**1** 0513 5.1 / 1203 0.6 / SA 1729 5.2 ●	**16** 0452 5.4 / 1136 0.3 / SU 1712 5.6 / ○ 2359 0.1	**1** 0018 0.7 / 0557 5.1 / TU 1234 0.8 / 1812 5.0	**16** 0024 0.2 / 0605 5.5 / W 1249 0.1 / 1829 5.4	**1** 0018 0.8 / 0609 5.1 / TH 1236 0.9 / 1824 4.9	**16** 0056 0.3 / 0635 5.4 / F 1322 0.2 / 1901 5.1
2 0014 0.4 / 0539 5.1 / F 1230 0.5 / 1754 5.3	**17** 0517 5.3 / 1157 0.4 / SA 1734 5.5	**2** 0021 0.5 / 0548 5.1 / SU 1235 0.6 / 1804 5.2	**17** 0539 5.5 / 1221 0.1 / M 1800 5.6	**2** 0045 0.8 / 0631 5.1 / W 1259 0.9 / 1844 4.9	**17** 0109 0.2 / 0651 5.4 / TH 1333 0.2 / 1915 5.2	**2** 0047 0.9 / 0641 5.0 / F 1305 0.9 / 1857 4.8	**17** 0140 0.4 / 0718 5.3 / SA 1405 0.4 / 1943 4.9
3 0051 0.4 / 0616 5.1 / SA 1304 0.5 / 1830 5.3	**18** 0020 0.2 / 0602 5.4 / SU 1241 0.2 / 1819 5.6	**3** 0051 0.6 / 0623 5.1 / M 1304 0.6 / 1837 5.1	**18** 0043 0.1 / 0625 5.5 / TU 1305 0.1 / 1846 5.5	**3** 0108 1.0 / 0701 5.0 / TH 1322 1.0 / 1914 4.8	**18** 0151 0.4 / 0734 5.3 / F 1415 0.5 / 2000 5.0	**3** 0116 1.0 / 0712 4.9 / SA 1335 1.0 / 1930 4.7	**18** 0221 0.6 / 0800 5.2 / SU 1447 0.6 / 2025 4.7
4 0122 0.6 / 0651 5.1 / SU 1334 0.7 / 1904 5.2	**19** 0103 0.1 / 0646 5.4 / M 1322 0.2 / 1904 5.5	**4** 0116 0.8 / 0656 5.1 / TU 1327 0.9 / 1908 5.0	**19** 0125 0.2 / 0709 5.4 / W 1346 0.2 / 1930 5.3	**4** 0133 1.1 / 0730 4.9 / F 1348 1.1 / 1945 4.6	**19** 0233 0.7 / 0817 5.1 / SA 1459 0.8 / 2045 4.6	**4** 0148 1.1 / 0745 4.8 / SU 1409 1.1 / 2005 4.5	**19** 0301 0.9 / 0840 4.9 / M 1529 0.9 / 2108 4.5

England

St Malo tides

ST MALO LAT 48°38'N LONG 2°02'W
TIMES AND HEIGHTS OF HIGH AND LOW WATERS

STANDARD TIME UT –01
Subtract 1 hour for UT
For French Summer Time add ONE hour in non-shaded areas

Dates in red are SPRINGS
Dates in blue are NEAPS

YEAR 2016

JANUARY		FEBRUARY		MARCH		APRIL	
Time m	Time m	Time m	Time m	Time m	Time m	Time m	Time m
1 0539 3.8 / 1109 9.9 / F 1801 3.9 / 2337 9.5	**16** 0555 2.6 / 1124 11.0 / SA 1823 2.7 / 2351 10.5	**1** 0610 4.3 / 1145 9.2 / M 1834 4.5 ◑	**16** 0019 10.0 / 0717 3.7 / TU 1257 9.6 / 1953 3.9	**1** 0531 3.9 / 1100 9.5 / TU 1750 4.2 / 2322 9.2	**16** 0653 3.7 / 1232 9.4 / W 1925 4.1	**1** 0648 4.6 / 1232 8.6 / F 1923 4.9	**16** 0210 9.0 / 0912 4.4 / SA 1509 9.0 / 2148 4.3
2 0617 4.3 / 1153 9.3 / SA 1843 4.4 ◑	**17** 0644 3.2 / 1219 10.3 / SU 1917 3.3	**2** 0018 8.8 / 0705 4.8 / TU 1249 8.7 / 1938 4.9	**17** 0133 9.4 / 0834 4.1 / W 1427 9.2 / 2116 4.1	**2** 0616 4.5 / 1148 8.9 / W 1842 4.8 ◑	**17** 0104 9.2 / 0808 4.3 / TH 1405 8.9 / 2051 4.5	**2** 0125 8.7 / 0818 4.6 / SA 1426 8.7 / 2106 4.6	**17** 0334 9.3 / 1031 3.9 / SU 1618 9.6 / 2257 3.7
3 0028 9.0 / 0709 4.7 / SU 1253 8.9 / 1941 4.7	**18** 0051 10.0 / 0746 3.7 / M 1328 9.8 / 2024 3.6	**3** 0142 8.6 / 0825 4.9 / W 1424 8.6 / 2110 4.8	**18** 0307 9.3 / 1006 4.0 / TH 1557 9.4 / 2243 3.8	**3** 0026 8.6 / 0723 4.9 / TH 1317 8.4 / 2005 5.0	**18** 0244 9.0 / 0945 4.3 / F 1542 9.2 / 2222 4.1	**3** 0308 9.1 / 0952 4.0 / SU 1549 9.5 / 2230 3.8	**18** 0434 10.0 / 1130 3.3 / M 1707 10.3 / 2350 3.1
4 0141 8.7 / 0820 4.9 / M 1411 8.8 / 2100 4.7	**19** 0207 9.7 / 0903 3.8 / TU 1451 9.7 / 2142 3.6	**4** 0315 8.8 / 0955 4.5 / TH 1548 9.0 / 2233 4.3	**19** 0427 9.9 / 1126 3.4 / F 1707 10.1 / 2353 3.1	**4** 0217 8.5 / 0902 4.7 / F 1507 8.7 / 2148 4.6	**19** 0407 9.6 / 1107 3.6 / SA 1648 9.9 / 2332 3.4	**4** 0419 10.1 / 1104 3.0 / M 1651 10.5 / 2336 2.8	**19** 0521 10.6 / 1217 2.7 / TU 1748 10.9

Central European Time is one hour ahead of GMT and on tide tables will be referred to as Standard Time UT–01.

Again, one hour is added during the summer months for daylight saving time.

About 70 countries currently observe daylight saving time. Equatorial and tropical countries tend not to. Where there is no difference in hours of daylight during the year there is no need to adjust clocks.

Despite being British, I will use the term UT for British standard time and DST for summer time, in an attempt to be international. UK almanacs are written this way and it would be confusing to keep insisting on GMT as opposed to UT.

14 Tidal heights

You need to know the height of tide to work out where you can anchor, when you can get over a sill or under a bridge, whether you will have enough water to sail over a drying height, if you will have enough anchor cable when you get to HW.

▶ *Getting over a sill.*

▼ *Getting on to a drying platform.*

i Handy tip

For ports where you might want to establish the height of tide manually on a regular basis, copy the tidal curve from the almanac, enlarge it to A4 and then laminate it in a matt laminate pouch. You can draw on these in pencil and rub out when you have finished.

▼ *Will you have enough anchor cable at HW?*

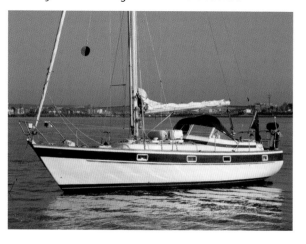

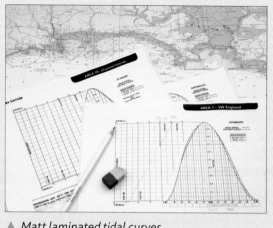

▲ *Matt laminated tidal curves.*

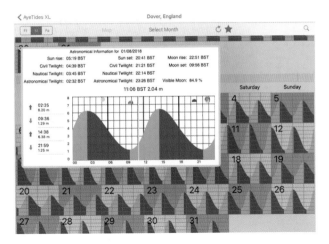

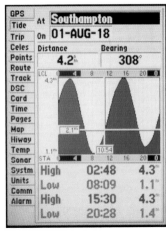

▲ AyeTides, Dover.

◀ *Garmin chart plotter tide, Southampton.*

▶ *Navionics tide information, Plymouth.*

The quickest way to find the height of tide is to look it up on your chart plotter or an app.

Or you can work it out for yourself with a tide table and a tidal curve.

And when you've done that you can check and see how closely the two match, your manual way versus the app. From experience, the two results will be very close.

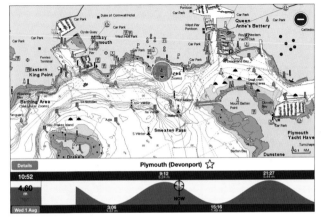

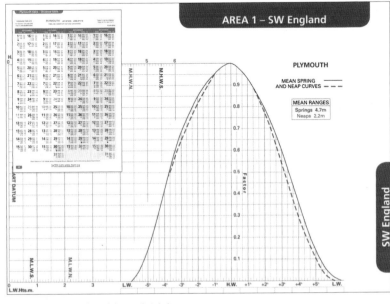

▲ *Plymouth tide table and tidal curve.*

Let's say you are in Plymouth.

You want to find the height of tide at 2006 on 16 September 2016 so you will use the Plymouth tide table and the Plymouth tidal curve.

First, check which tide the time 2006 will fall into. Will it be on an ebb tide or a flood tide? On 16 September there are two high waters – 0553UT and 1726UT. Remember, all times in the almanac are in the standard time of the country and you need to add one hour to these in the months of daylight saving time. So these two high waters will be 0653DST and 1826DST.

You are interested in the height of tide at 2006, which falls into the ebb tide from 1826 to 0026.

The height of HW at 1826 is shown as 5.6m and the LW height at 0026 is 0.6m.

Step 1 Go to the Plymouth tidal curve and fill in the HW time in the central box, 1826 and underneath it DST, so you know you converted it into your local time. Now write each hour in the boxes from 1826 to 0026.

Step 2 Mark the 5.6m on the top HW heights line and the 0.6m on the LW heights line at the bottom.

Step 3 Join these two up.

Step 4 Now you will see that there are two lines that you could work to. They are very similar in Plymouth. The blue dotted line is for neap tides and the solid red line is for spring tides.

Establish whether you are on springs or neaps by checking the range of the tide, the difference in height between HW and LW. Here 5.6 – 0.6m gives you a 5.0m range. To the right of the tidal curve is a box giving the mean ranges and you can see that the mean spring range is 4.7m so 5.0m is very much springs.

Step 5 You want the height of tide at 2006. And you will see that there are six intervals of ten minutes between each hour. So you go to the 2026 hour mark and move back two intervals to get 2006.

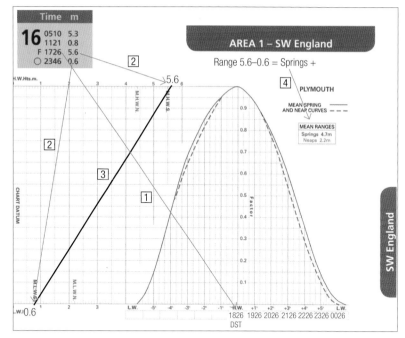

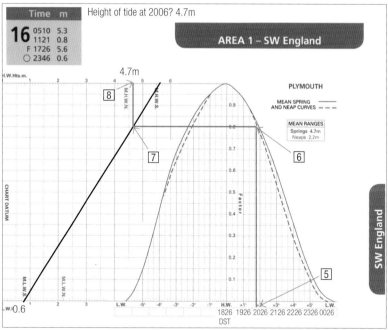

Step 6 Draw a line up from 2006 to where it cuts the red line.

Step 7 Draw a line across from here to the HW/LW line.

Step 8 Draw a line from here up to the top line, the HW heights line, and read off the height – 4.7m. This is the height of tide at 2006 on 16 September in Plymouth.

HOW ACCURATE ARE THE TIDAL HEIGHT APPS? VERY.

Here's a live check done on Sunday 29 July 2018 with AyeTides. Again Plymouth.

I drew it out on a tidal curve and came to 3.5m – just 2cm different from AyeTides. That'll do for me. Although tidal apps will give you the height to the nearest centimetre, working to one tenth of a metre is quite accurate enough.

▶ *AyeTides height of tide, Plymouth 1034 Sunday 29 July 2018 – 3.52m.*

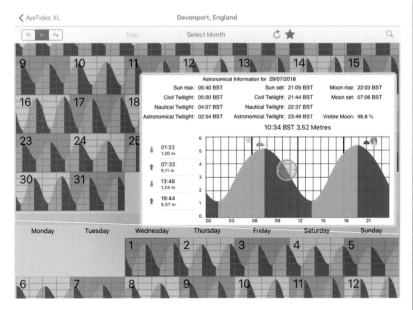

▶ *Drawn out on a tidal curve. HW Plymouth taken from the almanac 0735, so time taken as 1035 rather than 1 minute earlier at 1034 as shown on AyeTides above. What's a minute between friends?*

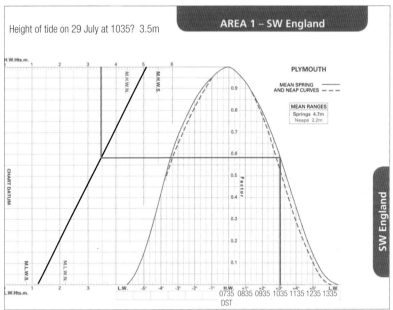

Rule of twelfths

A rough way of doing this is with 'the rule of twelfths'. Divide the range by 12.

LW

- In the 1st hour the tide rises by 1/12th.
- In the 2nd hour the tide rises by 2/12ths.
- In the 3rd hour the tide rises by 3/12ths.
- In the 4th hour the tide rises by 3/12ths.
- In the 5th hour the tide rises by 2/12ths.
- In the 6th hour the tide rises by 1/12th.

HW

The same principle applies from HW to LW. When you have a perfectly parabolic shaped tidal curve, the tide will ebb at the same rate as it floods.

Referring to your tide on 29 July 2018 with HW of 5.1m and LW of 1.2m, in a range of 3.9m, each one-twelfth would be 0.325m.

You wanted the height of tide at 1034, which was three hours after HW at 0735, give or take a minute. So you take 6/12ths: 1/12th from the first hour + 2/12ths from the second hour + 3/12ths from the third hour = 1.95m (half the range in this case) off the HW height of 5.1m to get a height at 1034 of 3.15m. That's only 35cm different from the actual answer so not a bad option if you simply had the times and heights of HW and LW and no app to refer to or tidal curve.

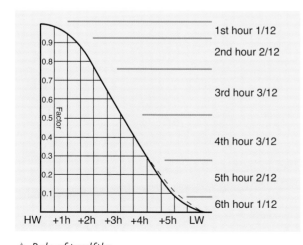

▲ *Rule of twelfths.*

This works only if the tidal curve is even, a parabolic curve. It wouldn't work for Portsmouth with its very uneven tidal curve, or Portland.

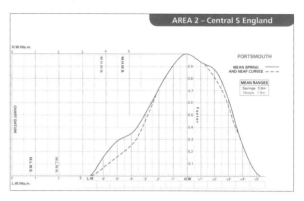

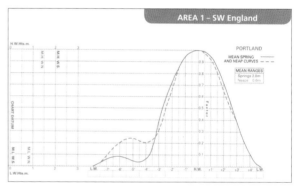

Using tidal information

1. To sail over a drying height or to get over a sill into a harbour

Say you have:

- a height of tide of 4.7m
- a draught (the amount of water you need to be afloat) of 1.5m
- a preferred under keel clearance (safety margin) of 1.5m.

You need 3.0m of water to float using your safety margin.

You have 4.7m of tide so you can safely sail over anything that is:

Height of tide	4.7m
Less draught	1.5m
Less safety margin	1.5m
	1.7m above chart datum

2. When anchoring

To find out what depth of water you need to anchor in now, to be afloat at LW:

Take the height of tide now.
Deduct the height of tide at LW.
This is the fall of the tide.

Add the fall of the tide to:
Your draught
Your desired under keel clearance...

...and if you anchor in this depth of water now, you will be afloat at LW with your desired under keel clearance (UKC).

Example:

Height of tide now	4.0m
− Height of tide at LW	1.5m
= Fall of tide	2.5m
+ Draught	1.5m
+ Under keel clearance	1.5m
= Total	5.5m

Anchor in 5.5m of water now and you will lose 2.5m as the tide ebbs to LW so you will have 3m of water of which you require 1.5m to float (your draught) and then you will be left with 1.5m (your safety margin), your preferred under keel clearance.

You can do this very easily using the tidal height apps. Here you are in Saint-Malo, France.

Height of tide at 1327	7.60m
Height of tide at LW	2.72m (LW at 1720)
Fall of tide	4.88m
Draught of your boat	1.50m
Desired minimum UKC	1.50m
Fall + draught + UKC	7.88m

Anchor now in 8.0m and you'll be afloat at LW 1720 with 1.62m (8.0m – 4.88m – 1.50m) under the keel.

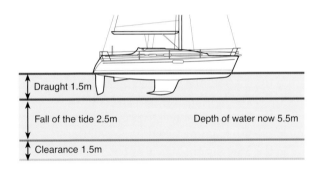

Boat now

Draught 1.5m

Fall of the tide 2.5m   Depth of water now 5.5m

Clearance 1.5m

Boat at low water

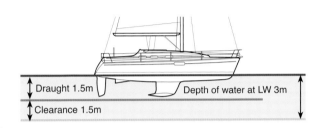

Draught 1.5m   Depth of water at LW 3m

Clearance 1.5m

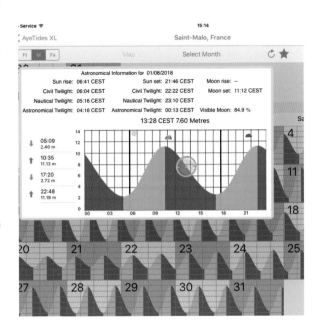

▶ *Height of tide at Saint-Malo.*

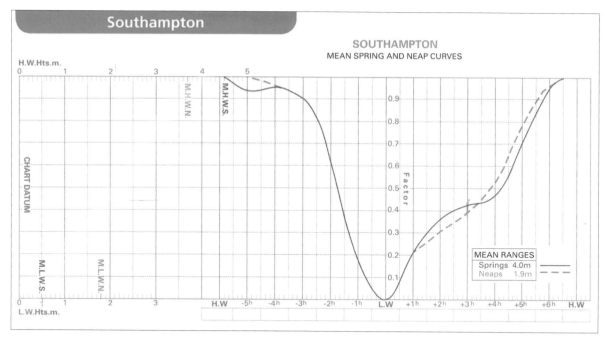

Southampton

SOUTHAMPTON
MEAN SPRING AND NEAP CURVES

MEAN RANGES	
Springs	4.0m
Neaps	1.9m

▲ *Southampton has a double HW and a stand on the flood. This is to do with a pinch point in the depth in the channel.*

Most Standard Ports have tidal curves that work off the HW. Southampton, however, works off the LW.

The key with tidal heights, whether you work them out yourself or whether you use tidal apps, is to understand:

1. That you add the height of tide to the chart datum sounding to get depth of water.

2. The 'fall of the tide', so that you always anchor in enough depth of water to be afloat with your desired under keel clearance at LW.

3. The 'rise of the tide' to ensure that you have enough anchor cable – chain and rope, or warp as it is called – to allow for the correct scope at HW.

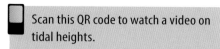

Scan this QR code to watch a video on tidal heights.

15

There are many ports and harbours around the world and it would be impossible for governments to provide a tide table for each one of them. So what they do is list 'Standard Ports' and then 'Secondary Ports' in between them with time and height differences that relate to the standard port.

If you are using an app or a chart plotter with tidal height information, you will probably not be aware of the secondary ports.

But when it comes to working them out manually, people – RYA Yachtmaster candidates in particular – seem to get themselves in a frightful pickle. And they are not that complicated. All you need to do is break the process down into simple steps.

Take Torquay, for example, which is referenced to the standard port of Plymouth. And it comes as no surprise to know that HW arrives later at Torquay, as the tide sweeps up the English Channel, it being to the east of Plymouth.

> **i** **In the UK, Ireland and the Channel Islands there are 32 standard ports**
>
> Falmouth, Plymouth, Dartmouth, Portland, Poole, Southampton, Portsmouth, Shoreham, Dover, Sheerness, London Bridge, Burnham-On-Crouch, Walton-On-The-Naze, Lowestoft, Immingham, River Tyne/North Shields, Leith, Aberdeen, Wick, Lerwick, Stornoway, Ullapool, Oban, Greenock, Liverpool (Alfred Dock), Holyhead, Milford Haven, Bristol (Avonmouth), Belfast, Galway, St Peter Port, St Helier.

The time difference is not the same for every time of HW at Plymouth, because the difference at Torquay varies according to whether you are dealing with a spring tide, where there is a lot of water sloshing about, or a neap tide, where there is less water flooding and ebbing.

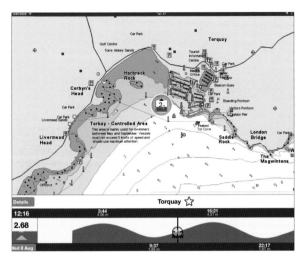

▲ This is Torquay, a secondary port. Its standard port is Plymouth. Here, all the secondary port workings have been done for you.

Torquay – River Exe

1.19 TORQUAY
Devon 50°27'·45N 03°31'·73W ✿✿✿✿✿✿✿✿ **1** 2a, b, c

CHARTS AC 3315, 1613, 5602, 26; Imray C5 **3**

TIDES –0500 Dover; ML 2·9; Duration 0640 **4**

Standard Port PLYMOUTH (←—) **5**

Times **6**				Height (metres) **7**			
High Water		Low Water		MHWS	MHWN	MLWN	MLWS
0100	0600	0100	0600	5·5	4·4	2·2	0·8
1300	1800	1300	1800				
Differences TORQUAY							
+0025	+0045	+0010	0000	–0·6	–0·7	–0·2	–0·1

NOTE: There is often a stand of about 1 hour at HW

▲ The Secondary Port information in the almanac is presented thus.

The almanac gives us a lot of information:

1. The latitude and longitude of Torquay

2. a. The red wheels tell you that it can be entered in any weather.
   b. The thumbs ups tell you it has good facilities for vessel and crew.
   c. The purple flowers tell you that it is an attractive place well worth visiting.

Torquay has the highest score you can get on all three counts. The almanac does say these ratings are naturally subjective.

3. These are the charts that cover Torquay.

4. Tides at Torquay occur 5 hours before Dover and the mean level is 2.9m, with an average tide duration of 6 hours 40 minutes.

5. The standard port for Torquay is Plymouth.

6. The time differences tell you:
   When HW Plymouth is 0100/1300, HW Torquay is +0025 (25 minutes later).
   When HW Plymouth is 0600/1800, HW Torquay is +0045 (45 minutes later).

These differences more or less coincide with the spring and neap tides, springs Plymouth are around 0600 and 1800 and neaps are around 0100 and 1300.

7. The height differences tell you:
   When HW Plymouth is 5.5m there is 0.6m less at Torquay.
   When HW Plymouth is 4.4m there is 0.7m less at Torquay.
   When LW Plymouth is 2.2m there is 0.2m less at Torquay.
   When LW Plymouth is 0.8m there is 0.1m less at Torquay.

LET'S WORK OUT AN EXAMPLE

On the day in question, HW Plymouth is 1600UT and the height of tide is 5.0m. LW is 2200UT with a height of 1.2m – you are looking at the ebb tide. You want to know what the time of HW at Torquay will be and the heights at Torquay of HW and LW.

First, find the time of HW at Torquay. For this, you will draw out a 'crocodile', as one of my students called it. Others might call it an interpolation diagram, but that sounds complicated so let's stick with crocodile.

Step 1 Draw a line across the page, which will be the time line.

Step 2 The HW Plymouth time of 1600 falls within the five-hour period of 1300 and 1800. So you need to mark off five intervals on your time line. You can do this by eye or with a ruler to get even spaces. By eye will be perfectly accurate enough. Mark off the hours and title this HW Plymouth UT. Bring this into Daylight Saving Time at the end if you need to.

Step 3 Draw a line at a 45° angle to this line. On this line, mark the time differences of HW at Torquay.

Step 4 The time differences run from +25 minutes at 1300 to +45 minutes at 1800. A range of 45–25 = 20 mins. So let's make these five intervals of 4 minutes each and mark these off on the differences line, starting with the +25 which matches up with the 1300, then +29, +33, +37, +41, +45.

Step 5 Join the time of 1800 with the offset of +0045.

As long as you work parallel to this line, the two scales, regardless of whether or not you used the same space for the intervals on each scale, will match up.

And you find that HW Plymouth at 1600 will be HW Torquay at 1637UT.

Now this is in the standard time of the country, here UT, and if you are in the summer months you need to bring it into Daylight Saving Time by adding one hour. And that is all there is to it.

What if you were not exactly on the hour, say HW Plymouth was 1730? Find 1730 on the time line and, working parallel to your 1800/+45min line, you find that the time difference is between +41min and +45min, midway. So that will be +43min. HW Plymouth 1730 is HW Torquay 1730 + 43 = 1813.

To establish the height differences, again use the crocodile, although here the differences do not change much between springs and neaps.

Reading from the Secondary Port information, you see that:

- At mean high water springs you take 0.6m off the Plymouth HW height for Torquay and at neaps you take off 0.7m.
- At mean low water springs we take 0.1m off the Plymouth LW height for Torquay and at neaps 0.2m.
- So there is very little difference in tide heights at Torquay, compared with its standard port of Plymouth.

If the HW or LW heights were exactly on springs or neaps I would use the figures given and if they were in between I would use the worst case figure of -0.7 for HW and -0.2 for LW, just to be safe.

On the day in the example, the HW Plymouth height of 5.0m is nearly halfway between the 5.5m and 4.4m ranges so I would err on the side of caution and use the -0.7, to give a HW height at Torquay of 4.3m.

For the LW height you have 1.2m at Plymouth, just under halfway between the 2.0 and 0.8m ranges so I would work to the -0.1, so LW height Torquay 1.2 – 0.1 = 1.1m.

My pencil is probably thicker than 0.1m on my tidal curve.

Now approach the Plymouth tidal curve with these figures:

HW Torquay   1637UT
HW height   4.3m
LW height   1.1m

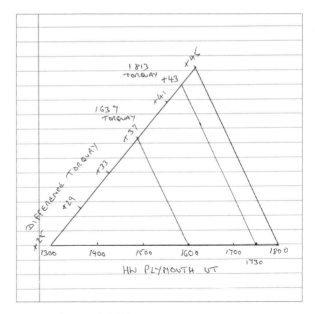

▲ *HW Plymouth 1730.*

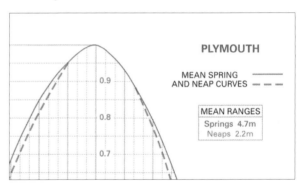

▲ *Plymouth mean ranges.*

To check that you are working to the correct line on the tidal curve, blue dotted neaps or red solid springs, check the range on the day. You had a HW Plymouth of 5.0m and a LW of 1.2m, range 3.8m, which is just over halfway between neaps and springs according to the mean ranges on the tidal curve (springs 4.7m, neaps 2.2m, midway 3.45m), so you will work to midway between the dotted blue and the solid red lines.

Let's say you want the height of tide at 1840UT. Go to the Plymouth tidal curve and lay on the information to get the height of tide at 1840UT of 3.6m.

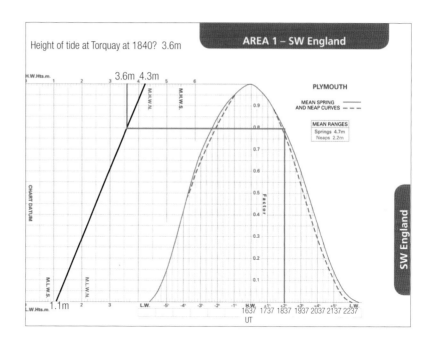

Height of tide at Torquay at 1840? 3.6m

3.6m 4.3m

PLYMOUTH

MEAN SPRING ——— AND NEAP CURVES – – –

MEAN RANGES
Springs 4.7m
Neaps 2.2m

1.1m

1637 1737 1837 1937 2037 2137 2237
UT

▶ *Height of tide, Torquay 1840 = 3.6m. It's actually 1837 but that's as close to 1840 as we can reasonably get on our tidal curve.*

HERE'S ANOTHER EXAMPLE: BRAYE HARBOUR IN ALDERNEY

You will see on page 106 that Braye is referenced to St Helier on Jersey and that while the HW time differences are not great, a range of only 10 minutes from 40 minutes after St Helier to 50 minutes after St Helier, the range of the heights is considerable: HW from 4.8m less at springs to 3.4m less at neaps, and LW from 1.5m less at neaps to 0.5m less at springs.

Looking at your chart plotters and apps, this is what you will see:

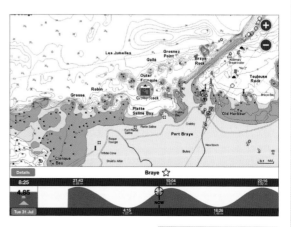

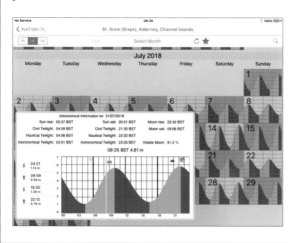

▲ *Navionics Braye. All the secondary port information has been worked out for you.*

▶ *My Garmin Braye – the same here.*

◀ *AyeTides – the same again.*

Low	04:15	1.2°
High	10:05	5.7°
Low	16:26	1.5°
High	22:16	5.8°

6.7 BRAYE HARBOUR

Alderney 49°43'·77N 02°11'·51W ✳✳✳♨♨♨♨♨♧♧

CHARTS AC 2669, 3653, 60, 2845, 5604.7/.8; SHOM 7158, 6934; Navi 1014; Imray C33A, 2500

TIDES –0400 Dover; ML 3·5; Duration 0545

Standard Port ST HELIER (→)

Times				Height (metres)			
High Water		Low Water		MHWS	MHWN	MLWN	MLWS
0300	0900	0200	0900	11·0	8·1	4·0	1·4
1500	2100	1400	2100				
Differences BRAYE							
+0050	+0040	+0025	+0105	−4·8	−3·4	−1·5	−0·5

They are giving us the height of tide at Braye at 0825 (DST). So, let's work out manually what they are telling us and see if we agree!

Braye Harbour is referenced to the standard port of St Helier in Jersey, so find the time of HW on 31 July 2018 at St Helier and the height of HW and height of LW.

HW St Helier is 0820UT, height 10.1m. The height of the LW before was 2.0m. You are on the flood tide.

Leave the time of HW St Helier in UT for now because the times of the secondary port differences are always in the standard time of the country. Once you have found the time of HW at Braye you will add one hour for DST and then write this on to your tidal curve.

Now the crocodile.

Step 1 Draw a line across the page, which will be the time line. And as 0820 falls within the range of 0300 and 0900, write out the six hours and title this HW St Helier UT.

Step 2 Draw a line at a 45° angle to this line for the time differences at Braye. These are from +50 minutes at 0300 to +40 minutes at 0900. A range of 50 − 40 = 10 minutes. So let's make these ten intervals of one minute each, starting with the +50, which matches up with the 0300, then running back to +40.

Step 3 Join the time of 0900 with the offset of +40 and work parallel to this line. Dividing the hour between 0800 and 0900 into three parts, find 0820. This meets the differences line at +41 minutes.

Step 4 When HW St Helier is 0820UT, HW Braye is 0901UT.

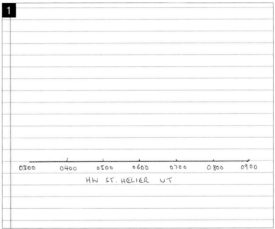

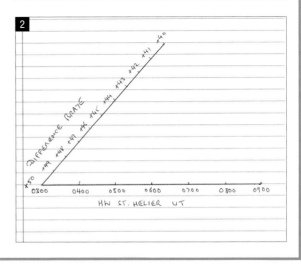

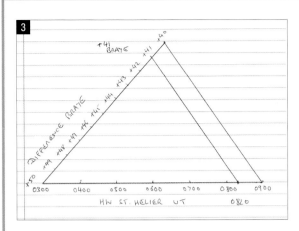

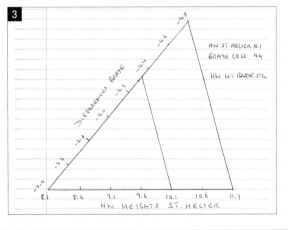

As you are in July, add one hour to this to bring it into DST: HW St Helier 0820UT, HW Braye 1001DST.

To establish the height differences, again use the crocodile.

Looking at the Braye secondary port detail, there are significant height differences at Braye between spring tides and neap tides compared with St Helier.

When HW St Helier is 11.0m, there will be 4.8m less of tide at Braye and when HW St Helier is 8.1m, there will be 3.4m less tide at Braye.

HW St Helier is 10.1m, so what is the height of HW at Braye?

Use your crocodile.

Step 1 Again draw a line and mark off the range of the HW St Helier heights. You have 8.1m to 11m, which does not divide nicely, so you will go in 0.5m intervals from 8.1m to 11.1m – as I've said before, my pencil is probably thicker than 0.1m when drawing on the tidal curve.

Step 2 Draw a line at 45° to this and mark off the height differences. The range of this is from -3.4m to -4.8m so you can divide these into six intervals of 0.2m.

Step 3 Having joined 11.1m and 4.8m and working parallel to this line, you find that 10.1m or near enough gives you a height difference of just over midway between -4.2m and -4.4m, so allow -4.4m.

So when HW height St Helier is 10.1m, HW height Braye is 10.1m – 4.4m = 5.7m.

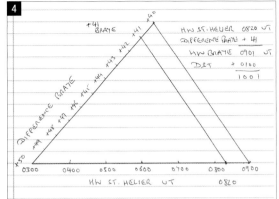

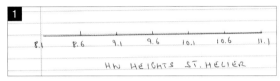

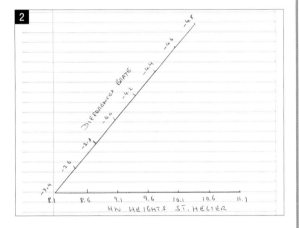

And when the LW height at St Helier is 1.4m you will have 0.5m less at Braye.

Step 1 On your crocodile, mark off the LW heights on the line in 0.5m intervals from 1.5m to 4.0m.

Step 2 Draw a line at 045° with the differences from 0.5m to 1.5m in 0.2m intervals.

Step 3 Connect 4.0m on the heights line to -1.5m on the differences line and, working parallel to this, find that with an LW height at St Helier of 2.0m you will have 0.70m less at Braye. LW height Braye 2.0m – 0.7m = 1.3m.

Now place this information on to the St Helier tidal curve.

HW Braye 1001DST
Height 5.7m
LW before height 1.3m

Work to the red line because the St Helier range on the day was 8m and this is pretty close to the spring range of 9.6m. In any event, it makes no difference because at the time you are working there is only the red curve to work to.

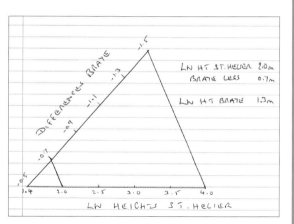

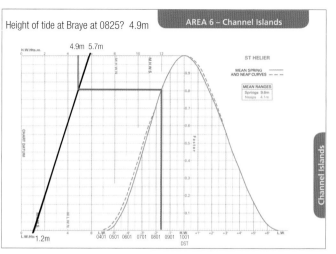

So how did that compare with the programs and apps?

You were spot on with the tide programs and apps. As long as you ensure that you have a sufficient safety margin under the keel – at least one metre for me – then you will always be safe.

As you've probably worked out by now, secondary ports are not hard, there are just logical steps you need to take. And, of course, you can do them in your head. You just take the figures for the range of times and the range of differences and 'normalise' them.

If you have a difference that runs from -0012 when HW at the standard port is 0000/1200 and +0012 when HW is at 0600/1800, you can see that you have

By hand and by app: a comparison				
	By hand	Navionics	AyeTides	Garmin
HW Braye	1001	1004	0959	1005
HW Ht Braye	5.7m	5.66m	5.59m	5.7m
LW Ht Braye	1.3m	1.22m	1.13m	1.2m
Height at 0825DST	4.9m	4.85m	4.81m	4.8m

six hours of difference and a range of 24 minutes of difference. Divide the difference (24) by the hours (6) and each hour you move along the time line from 0000 to 0600, the difference moves by 4 minutes.

	0000	0100	0200	0300	0400	0500	0600
	1200	1100	1000	0900	0800	0700	
		1300	1400	1500	1600	1700	1800
	0000	2300	2200	2100	2000	1900	
Difference	-12	-8	-4	0	+4	+8	+12

Times of HW	0000	0600
Times of HW	1200	1800
Differences	+0012	-0012

Every hour you move along the time line from 0000 to 0600, you move 4 minutes from -12 to +12.

So if HW at the standard port is 0200 then HW at your secondary port will be -12 minutes + 2 x 4 minutes (8 minutes) = -4 minutes, so 0156.

If HW at the standard port was 1630, then HW at your secondary port would be 1636. Start at the 1800 end of the scale and move 6 minutes along your differences line (being 4 minutes for 1 hour of time and 2 minutes for 30 minutes of time), to get +0012 less 6 mins = +6 minutes, so HW secondary port 1636.

Do the same for the height differences.

Quite often, secondary port time differences are the same for springs and neaps, although this will not be the case in any exam.

Of course, if you are taking a navigation exam, then drawing out a 'crocodile' is the way for me, regardless of whether you are at RYA Day Skipper, Yachtmaster or Officer of the Watch level.

Before we leave secondary ports, let's tie secondary ports and tidal heights together with a real example.

Calamity! The anchor snagged yesterday just as you were leaving your favourite bay near Newlyn and you had to leave it behind. Today you want to go back and dive down to collect it. You had anchored on a drying height, which is why you had to get away yesterday and leave the anchor behind, as the tide was ebbing.

The spot dries by 2.0m. Your boat draws 1.5m and you'll need a minimum under keel clearance of

9.1.8   NEWLYN

Cornwall 50°06'·19N 05°32'.58W ✳✳⚓⚓⚓✿✿

CHARTS AC 777, 2345; Imray C7, 2400.10; Stanfords 2; OS 203

TIDES −0635 Dover; ML 3·2; Duration 0555; Zone 0 (UT)

Standard Port PLYMOUTH (⟶)

Times				Height (metres)			
High Water		Low Water		MHWS	MHWN	MLWN	MLWS
0000	0600	0000	0600	5·5	4·4	2·2	0·8
1200	1800	1200	1800				
Differences NEWLYN							
−0040	−0110	−0035	−0025	+0·1	0·0	−0·2	0·0

▲ *Newlyn Secondary Port Information – note this is from 2007. Differences can change from year to year. Always check your almanac for current information.*

0.5m just to be safe. So you will need 4.0m of tide to get back to the anchor. You marked the spot on the chart plotter and tied a fender to the chain so you should be able to find it easily.

You want to do this in daylight.

The details:
The standard port for Newlyn is Plymouth.
Date: 7 October 2018
LW Plymouth   1021UT   1.1m
HW Plymouth   1621UT   5.5m
LW Plymouth   2248UT   0.7m

You need to know when you can get on to the spot and by what time you will have to leave. In other words, when will you have 4m of tide at that spot?

Retrieving your anchor

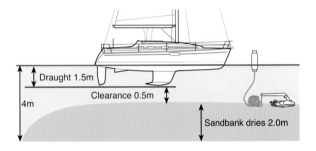

Step 1 Find HW Newlyn by crocodile or in your head. The time differences go from -40 minutes at 1200 to -70 minutes (-0110) at 1800, a range of 30 minutes. So each hour you move along the time line from 1200 by 5 minutes from -0040 towards -0110.

Doing a crocodile tells you that when HW Plymouth is 1621, HW Newlyn is 61 minutes earlier. You can do this in your head, too.

When HW Plymouth is 1621UT, HW Newlyn is 1520UT. But you are in early October so add an hour for DST. HW Newlyn 1620DST.

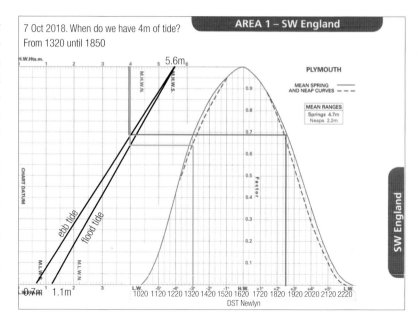

Step 2 Height differences. HW 5.5m. Plymouth has +0.1 added to it for Newlyn to make it 5.6m.

The first LW at 1.1m is closer to 0.8m than 2.2m so leave it alone. The same goes for the second LW at 0.7m. No change to the LW heights.

Step 3 Now place this information on the tidal curve for Plymouth.

HW Newlyn	1620DST
1st LW	1.1m
HW	5.6m
2nd LW	0.7m

Step 4 If you follow the line down from 4m and draw a line across from the first tide (1.1m to 5.6, the flood tide) to where it cuts the spring line (the ranges of these two tides are both springs) and then follow down, you will find the time you will have 4.0m on the flood tide.

Do the same for the ebb tide from 5.6m to 0.7m.

And you find that you can get on with 0.5m under keel clearance at 1320 and must be away by 1850.

That's easy when you have a chart plotter. Just move the cursor to give you instant answers. AyeTides tells you that you will have 4.0m at 1358 and must be away by 1900.

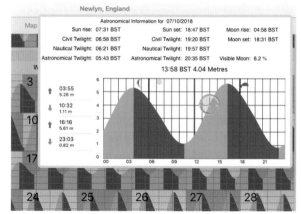

▲ *On at 1358.*

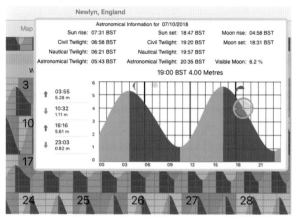

▲ *Off by 1900.*

Well, aim to get there ready for 1320 and see if you can get on. But still aim to be off before 1850.

By the way, to remind yourself that you can do secondary ports in your head, here are the tidal times and height for Newlyn and its standard port Plymouth at 1155 on 8 August 2018.

Notice that HW Plymouth is 1540BST and that HW Newlyn is 1444BST?

Yes, AyeTides use the expression British Summer Time. It's the same as Daylight Saving Time, one hour ahead of UT.

Let's check that. Referring to the secondary port information for Newlyn above, you know that the difference at 1200UT between Plymouth and Newlyn is -0040 and that each hour you move along the time line is 5 minutes along the differences line. Bring 1540BST into UT by taking an hour off to get 1440. This is 2 hours 40 minutes along the time line from 1200, so roughly 2.66 × 5 minutes, which is about 13 minutes. 13 minutes along from -0040 gives you -0053 from the 1440UT = 1347. Add an hour to get back to BST/DST gives you 1447.

AyeTides tells you that HW Newlyn is 1444. That's close enough for me.

Of course, working with the apps and programs is so much faster than doing it by hand, but it's good to know that you can check what you are being told if you want to.

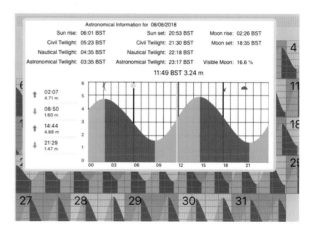

▲ Newlyn.

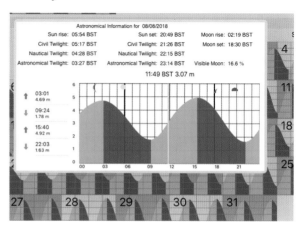

▲ Plymouth.

▶ This is the thinking that you will be doing.

Scan this QR code to watch a video on secondary ports.

Newlyn to Plymouth secondary port calculation 'In our heads'

6 hours – 1200 to 1800
30 mins of difference (40 mins to 70 mins)
30 ÷ 6 = 5 mins along the difference line for each hour we move along the time line

Time of HW Plymouth

1200	1300	1400	1440 1500	1600	1700	1800
-0040	-0045	-0050	-0055	-0060	-0065	-0070
-5 mins	-5 mins	-5 mins	-5 mins	-5 mins	-5 mins	

Difference Newlyn

1440: 2 lots of -5 mins from 1200 to 1400 = -10 mins
plus 66% of 5 mins for the 40 mins = approx -3 mins
-0040 and -0013 make -0053
HW Plymouth 1440 -53 mins = HW Newlyn 1347 UT

16 Sailing

Points of sail

Sailing boats will not sail directly into the wind. In fact, there is a 'no go' area roughly 45° either side of the bow. If you sail inside this area you will find that the boat slows and stalls and you are in 'stays' or in 'irons'. You have luffed up. The front edge of the sails, the luff, is pointing dead into the wind, the sails are flapping and you have no control over the boat. You need to come off the wind by bearing away on one tack or the other until the boat picks up speed and you regain control.

You will notice in the 'Points of Sail' diagram on page 116 that the starboard tack is coloured green and the port tack red. This is to remind you that when you are on starboard tack the wind is coming across the boat from the starboard side, where your green navigation sidelight will be. The boat will be heeling to port.

When you are on port tack the wind will be coming over the port side of the boat where your red navigation sidelight will be and you will be heeling to starboard.

Knowing which tack you are on is extremely important because it is the basis of the collision rules.

In a crossing situation between two sailing boats, the boat on starboard tack is the stand-on vessel and the boat on port tack is the give-way vessel.

Tacking and gybing

Tacking is when you take the bows of the boat through the wind and change from one tack to another.

For me, the call from the helm is: 'Ready about?'

If the helmsman hears no complaint from the crew, he turns the boat towards the wind by turning the helm to windward or putting the tiller down to leeward and as he does so calls: 'Lee ho!'

---

i Lee bowing

By sailing on the tack that has the tide on your lee side you will sail closer to the wind and make better progress towards your destination than if you have the tide on your windward side. Always be aware of the preferred tack.

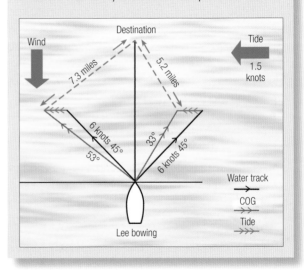

Lee bowing

Gybing is when you take the stern of the boat through the wind and gybe from one tack to another.

For me, the call from helm is:

'Stand by to gybe?'

If the helmsman hears no complaint from the crew, he turns the boat away from the wind by turning the helm to leeward or bringing the tiller up to windward and as he does so calls: 'Gybe ho!'

Nice and straightforward. If having been informed by the helmsman that they are to tack or gybe and any member of crew has a problem, they should shout out clearly, so that the helmsman will hold the manoeuvre until they are ready.

True wind and apparent wind

'True wind' is the wind you experience if you are standing still and 'apparent wind' is the wind you experience when moving through the water.

As you sail along, you bring the apparent wind forward towards the bow and it increases in speed over the true wind.

However, on the water our true wind is made up of the tide wind (whose strength and direction is equal and opposite to the tidal flow) and the ground wind, which is the wind you would feel onshore. Your motion wind (equal and opposite to your speed through the water), combined with the true wind equals your apparent wind, the wind you experience on the boat.

Modern instrument systems will switch between true wind and apparent wind direction and speed. Older instruments may well only read apparent wind speed and direction.

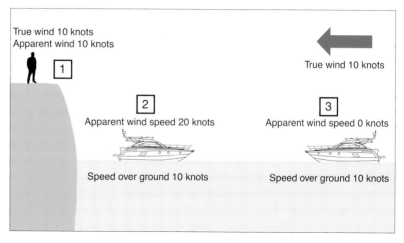

▲ True and apparent wind speed, assuming there is no tide.

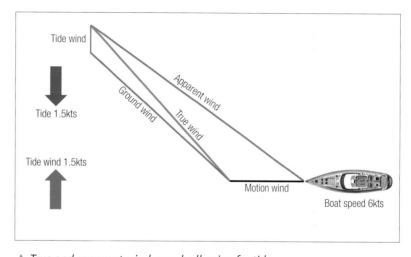

▲ True and apparent wind speed, allowing for tide.

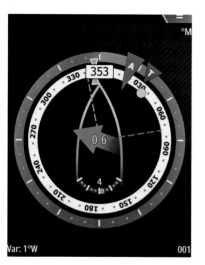

◀ B&G SailSteer showing heading, apparent wind angle, true wind angle and set and rate of the tide.

True wind from apparent wind the manual way

You can work out the angle and speed of the true wind you are experiencing on the boat from your apparent wind by drawing it on a piece of paper.

Step 1 Draw a vertical line. The bottom of the line is your boat.

Step 2 From the bottom of the line, draw the apparent wind angle and mark off the apparent wind speed in a convenient scale – such as 1 knot to 1 cm.

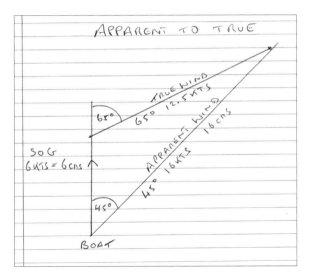

▲ *Apparent to true wind angle and speed.*

Step 3 Mark off your speed on your vertical line. Say 6 knots, so 6cm.

Step 4 Join this point with the end of the apparent wind line.

The angle of this line is the angle of the true wind and the length is the true wind speed.

Laying the windward mark

Racers need to know when to tack to make the mark to windward. Tack too early and they will end up downtide of it and have to put in another tack to make it. Too late and they will end up unnecessarily uptide of the mark. The rest of us need this same

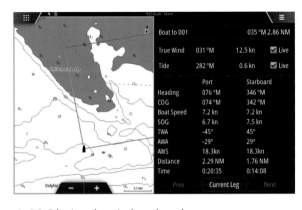

▲ *B&G laying the windward mark.*

information to know when to tack to make the headland, for example, or to make a waypoint.

Of course, there are programs on your plotter that can tell you this. Here, the B&G SailSteer program shows you the layline and it is constantly updating, allowing for the fluctuations of the wind and the strengthening and weakening of the tide. It is doing a vast number of complex arithmetical sums that you couldn't hope to keep pace with.

But you can work the layline out for yourself if you don't have a gizmo to do it for you.

In this example, you are on starboard tack making 5 knots. The wind is from the north and you are close-hauled. You want to know when to tack on to port to clear the west cardinal marking the shallows at Hand Deeps, just to the west of Eddystone Lighthouse. The tide is setting 180°T 1.5 knots.

Step 1 Establish the position now and mark it on the chart, with a dot with a circle round and the time. This is A.

Step 2 Take the heading according to the steering compass, convert it into °M by allowing for deviation and then into °T by allowing for magnetic variation. This gives you 315°T, but you estimate that you are experiencing 5° of leeway – wind on starboard pushing you negatively around the compass.

Step 3 Draw in the heading, the water track of 315°T − 5° = 310°T.

Step 4 Mark 5 miles off down this line – your boat speed. This is your dead reckoning position in an hour's time. This is B.

Step 5 From B, draw in the tide line – 1.5 miles at 180°T. This is C. This is actually where you will be in one hour's time.

Step 6 Now draw the tide from above the west cardinal back to it, 1.5 miles at 180°T.

Step 7 You will tack through 90°, which means your true heading on port tack will be 315° plus

90°, which is 045°. But you will also experience 5° of leeway now on the port side pushing you positively around the compass so you draw back from the start of this tide line a bearing of 050° and mark off 5 miles down this line.

Step 8 Join the 5-mile mark up with the west cardinal – this is your layline – and extend this line until it cuts your current course over ground.

This is the point at which you can tack on to port and make the windward mark. (I have allowed for deviation and magnetic variation and given you the courses in °T.)

You can establish when this point to tack will occur by taking the distance A – to where the layline line cuts your COG (2.4 miles) ÷ the distance AC (4.2 miles) × 60. In this instance, about 34 minutes.

Of course, if you have a chart plotter that's giving you heading and COG, you can predict the layline.

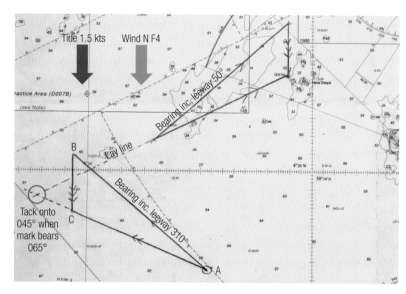

▲ *Laying the windward mark.*

Current heading 315°T gives you a COG of 294°T, a difference of 21°. Your new heading will be 315° plus 90° for your tacking angle, plus 21° (the difference between heading and COG) = 66°T. Set a distance and bearing mark from you to the cardinal and when it bears 066°, tack and steer 045°T.

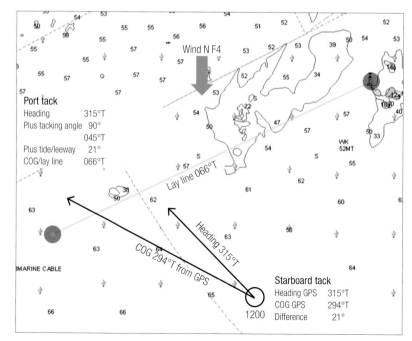

▲ *Layline by GPS COG.*

> **i** Handy tip:
> ## Tack on a header
>
> - When the wind shifts towards the bow you are being 'headed'.
> - When the wind shifts towards the stern you are being 'freed'.
> - Racers generally tack on a 'header' as this keeps them sailing more directly to the next mark.
> - So, if you are headed, tack and you will make your upwind destination that much quicker.

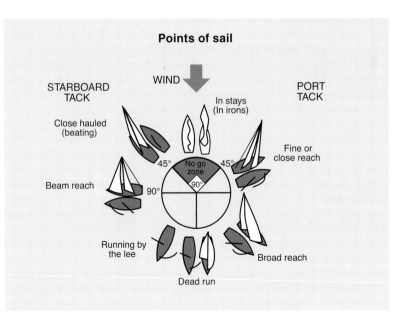

Points of sail

WIND

STARBOARD TACK

PORT TACK

In stays (In irons)

Close hauled (beating)

Fine or close reach

45° No go zone 45° 90°

Beam reach 90°

Running by the lee

Broad reach

Dead run

ℹ Glossary

- Goose winged or wing and wing – when you are sailing dead downwind with the headsail out on one side and the mainsail out on the other.

- Leeward (pronounced looward) – the leeward side of the vessel is the side where the wind is going to.

- Reaching – when the wind is on the beam.

- Downwind sailing – you will be on anything from a broad reach (wind 120°) to dead downwind (wind 180°) or even by the lee (wind beyond 180°).

- Sailing by the lee – when you have the wind on the same side as that on which the mainsail is set. You can control this if the wind is just on the same side of the mainsail, but anything more than a few degrees and you run the risk of the main gybing over unexpectedly and violently. A crash gybe is to be avoided.

- Windward – the windward side of the vessel is the side the wind is coming from.

- Windward sailing – you will be on a fine or close reach or close-hauled, beating to windward.

Aids to navigation

There are many apps you can download to help you learn and identify the aids to navigation, but here are a few pointers.

Buoyage

There are six types of navigation buoy or beacon. And they all have distinctive colours, top marks and lights. Taking them in the order that you will come across them as you arrive at a port, there are:

Safe water marks

These tell you where the safe water is. You can pass them on either side, but by convention you leave them to port. This will place you on the right-hand side of the channel, the correct side as you enter port.

Lateral marks

These mark the port and starboard sides of the navigable channel.

Colour   Red to port (IALA A) flat topped
              Green to starboard (IALA A) conical.

This is reversed for IALA Region B – green to port, flat topped and red to starboard, conical.

Cardinal marks

There are four cardinal marks, reflecting the four cardinal points of the compass – north, east, south, west – and they guide you round dangers. They indicate the direction of the safe water. North cardinal? The safe water is to the north of it.

▲ *Safe water mark. Light white – long flashing, occulting, isophase or Morse letter A.*

▶ **North cardinal**: 2 cones pointing up.
Colour: black at the top, yellow at the bottom.
Light: white uninterrupted flashing.

▲ **West cardinal**: 2 cones pointing towards each other.
Colour: yellow at the top, black in the middle and yellow at the bottom.
Light: white 9 flashes in the sequence.

▼ **East cardinal**: 2 cones pointing away from each other.
Colour: black at the top, yellow in the middle and black at the bottom.
Light: white 3 flashes in the sequence.

◀ **South cardinal**: 2 cones pointing down.
Colour: yellow at the top, black at the bottom.
Light: white 6 short and 1 long flash in the sequence

▶ *The Cardinals.*

Interestingly, in general the USA does not use cardinal marks. However, where the waters are state controlled and there is no federal jurisdiction it does have cardinals, although they don't follow the international rules. The USA tends to rely on lateral buoyage and is not that fussed about the shape of the top marks; it seems to rely on colour to navigate. Tough if you are colour blind.

Isolated danger marks

As the name suggests, they mark dangers in places you might not expect. The post or body will be coloured black with one or more red bands around it. The top mark is two black balls and the light will flash twice within the sequence.

Special marks

These can mark anything from a water skiing area to a serious danger. They are also used as racing marks and are often seasonal. The top mark is an X and they are yellow. If lit, the light will be yellow.

▲ *The USA often relies on colour rather than shape to distinguish between port and starboard markers.*
PHOTO: MONIQUE VAN SOMEREN

Emergency wreck marking buoys

These mark a recent wreck and will be removed once the wreck has either been removed or has been given the appropriate marks and chart position to warn sailors of the danger. The top mark is a cross and they are blue and yellow.

◀ *Emergency wreck marking buoy. The light will be alternating yellow and blue.*

▼ *Special mark by the SS* Richard Montgomery *US Liberty Ship that foundered on the Nore Bank in the Thames Estuary in 1944. It still has 21,400 tons of explosives onboard.*

▲ *Here is an isolated danger in the middle of Chichester harbour.*

▼ *Racing buoy.*

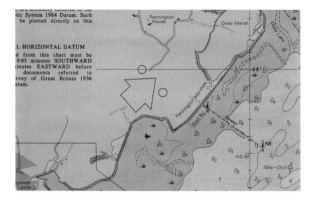

▲ *Direction of buoyage arrow, standard.*

▶ *Direction of buoyage arrow on colour paper charts and raster charts.*

The direction of navigation is always from seaward towards the port. Direction of navigation is marked on a chart with a large arrow with two circles ahead of it.

How to tell if a buoy or charted mark is lit

A light will have a teardrop. On vector charts the lights will have a teardrop the same colour as that of the light, except that white lights have a magenta teardrop.

Raster charts, being copies of the paper chart, will follow the paper chart.

Older UK Hydrographic Office paper charts give lights a magenta teardrop, whatever the colour of the light. Newer colour charts give lights teardrops the same colour as the light, except that white lights have yellow teardrops.

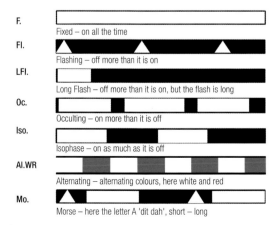

F.	Fixed – on all the time
Fl.	Flashing – off more than it is on
LFl.	Long Flash – off more than it is on, but the flash is long
Oc.	Occulting – on more than it is off
Iso.	Isophase – on as much as it is off
Al.WR	Alternating – alternating colours, here white and red
Mo.	Morse – here the letter A 'dit dah', short – long

▲ *The way a light can show itself.*

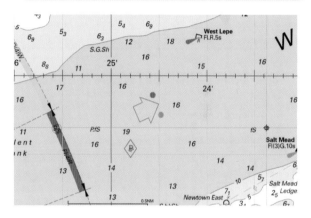

i ### Pontoon attached to the land

At night a pontoon attached to the land will be lit with two fixed lights vertically, one above the other, red for port and green for starboard in IALA system A. The light will be described as 2F.R(vert).

▲ *Pontoon attached to the land.*

How to remember the colour of the post on an isolated danger mark

Think of Dennis the Menace's T shirt – black and red stripes. The top mark will be two black balls and if lit it will flash (white) two in the sequence.

Within lateral marks there are also preferred channel markers. There are occasions when a main channel has another channel beside it and to indicate the main channel the lateral mark will have a band round it. Take the River Hamble, there is a preferred channel marker at the start of the river, because while there is a channel to port of the main channel for those who are going to Hamble Point Marina and the Hamble river moorings, the main channel is to starboard of this and, falling within IALA A, the red port-hand marker has a green stripe round, indicating that the preferred channel is to

THE DIFFERENCE BETWEEN A BEACON AND A BUOY

- A beacon is fixed in the ground or seabed.

- A buoy is floating.

- On a vector chart, both will be shown vertically – you click on the mark to find out if it is a buoy or a beacon.

- On a raster chart, being a copy of the paper chart, a beacon will be shown vertically and a buoy tilted to one side.

▶ *Two leading beacons in Salcombe and one red buoy, a port-hand marker.*

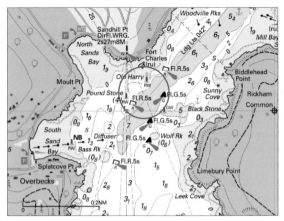

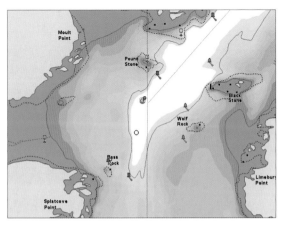

▲ *A vector chart (Navionics) showing the buoys and beacons, vertically. Interrogate for more detail.*

▲ *Raster chart from Imray Navigator showing the two beacons and the buoy.*

starboard. Light sequence will be two flashes, followed by a single flash after a pause, and the colour of the light will be red. This is a good reminder that it is always important to watch a light over a couple of sequences to make sure you have identified it correctly.

▶ *You can go to port of this mark, but the preferred channel is to starboard.*

HANDY WAY TO REMEMBER THE CARDINALS

North cardinal – both cones point north. And if you think of the point of the cone representing black and the wide part representing yellow, then it is easy to see that it will be coloured black at the top and yellow at the bottom.

East cardinal – the cones pointing away from each other give you a colour scheme of black yellow black. Think of this as the yellow yolk of an egg. E for egg, E for east.

South cardinal – both cones are facing south and it is yellow at the top and black at the bottom.

West cardinal – the two cones facing towards each other give you a colour scheme of yellow black yellow. I have heard some people say that you can recognise the top mark by looking at it sideways and seeing a 'W'. One of my students said that she remembered the colours of yellow black yellow because a lady of a certain age would always want to wear a dark colour around her waist and this waist reminded her of the W of the west cardinal.

▲ *Post covered in guano, fortunately the top mark tells you it is a north cardinal – two cones facing up.*

▶ *Here the top mark is missing, but the buoy is yellow at the top and black at the bottom so it is a south cardinal.*

Lights

Lighthouses

They warn of a danger – a headland, rocks – and can be seen from great distances: Portland Bill (England) 25 miles, Cape May (Delaware, USA) 24 miles, Cape Otway (Australia) 25 miles.

The light sequence will be written like this:
Fl(2)15s.58m18M

meaning flashing twice in 15 seconds. The focal plane of the light is 58 metres above MHWS, the white light nominally visible for 18 miles.

▲ *Portland Bill lighthouse.*

Lighthouses may also have a horn that will sound in fog, which will be written like this: Horn(1)60s, meaning the horn will sound once every 60 seconds.

Sectored lights

Sectored lights let you know the safe sector. In the red sector you are too far to port, in the green sector too far to starboard. You need to be in the white sector to follow the navigable channel.

The light sequence will be written in this order:
Fl(3)WRG.15s20m10M-8M

meaning flashing three times in 15 seconds. The height of the focal plane of the lights is 20 metres above MHWS. Nominal range of visibility of the lights: white 10 miles, green 8 miles and red somewhere in between 8 and 10 miles.

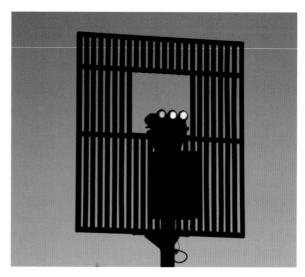

▲ *Sectored light.*

Light vessels

These vessels mark dangers or give warnings, like the Channel Light Vessel at the western end of the Casquets Traffic Separation Scheme. However, today not many of these lights are on actual vessels around the UK.

Calshot Spit marks the edge of a sandbank in the Solent and is no longer a ship but a floating structure. It is still anchored and therefore classed as a vessel with an anchor ball by day and an anchor light by night, plus its white warning light, which flashes every 5 secs – Fl.5s.

▲ *Light vessel. Notice the anchor ball in the bow, it tells you which way the tide is running.*

▲ *Approaching the transit.*

▲ *On the transit, follow this line.*

Transits

When two marks come into line they are 'in transit'. If they are charted you can draw a bearing line on the chart and you know you are somewhere down this line. A cross bearing or a depth will help to give you a position. But in terms of navigation, transits are used widely to help you navigate safely. They may be objects in line, or marks in line or lights in line.

▶ *Get these diamonds to line up to enter port safely.*

The International Regulations for the Prevention of Collisions at Sea 1972 (Colregs) state at Rule 5:

Every vessel shall at all times maintain a proper look-out by sight and hearing as well as by all available means appropriate in the prevailing circumstances and conditions so as to make a full appraisal of the situation and of the risk of collision.

Additionally they state six factors that mariners need to consider in relation to safe speed:

1. Visibility
2. Traffic density
3. Manoeuvrability of the vessel
4. Presence of background lights at night, which can confuse
5. State of the sea, wind, current and proximity of navigational hazards
6. The draught of the vessel in relation to the depth of water.

If the compass bearing of another ship does not change appreciably and you are closing, then a risk of collision exists.

▲ *The big chap is constrained by draught so the little chap must keep out of its way – you can just see a black cylinder on the aft mast of the tanker (Constrained by Draught – cylinder by day).*

Who gives way to whom?

You need to know if you are the stand-on or give-way vessel. Even if you are the stand-on vessel, if you see that the give-way vessel is not giving way then you must do everything possible to avoid a collision.

In confined waters I keep well out of the way of big ships. You are not allowed to enter narrow channels or precautionary areas when big ships are navigating them, but even when they have moved into freer water I will keep out of the way. In open water at sea I tend to stand on if I am under sail because that is what the big ship will expect you to do. Often at night they will flash me with a light to let me know they have seen me – at least, that's what I think they mean!

> **? Who gives way to whom – the pecking order**
>
> - A motorboat (power-driven by an engine via a propeller or jet propelled)
>
> gives way to
> - a rowing boat (power driven by man via an oar and rowlock)
>
> gives way to
> - a sailing boat
>
> gives way to
> - a fishing vessel or trawler
>
> gives way to
> - a vessel constrained by draught
>
> gives way to
> - a vessel restricted in her ability to manoeuvre
>
> gives way to
> - a vessel not under command.

The order of ascendancy in stand-on and give-way starts with sailing.

A yacht on port tack (with the wind coming over the port side) gives way to a yacht on starboard tack (with the wind coming over the starboard side).

▲ *Different tacks. Port tack gives way to starboard tack.*

When two yachts are on the same tack, the windward yacht – the one closer to the wind – gives way to the downwind yacht.

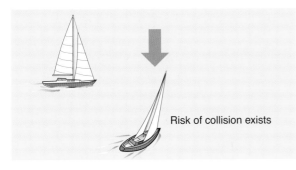

▲ *Same tack, windward yacht gives way.*

An overtaking vessel shall keep out of the way until it is past and clear. Overtaking is defined as 'coming with another vessel from a direction more than 22.5° abaft its beam'.

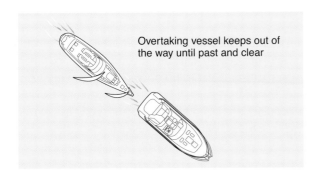

Power head on

When two power-driven vessels are approaching each other head on, they both need to turn to starboard and pass port to port.

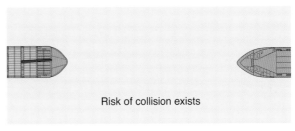

▲ *Both vessels turn to starboard. Sound signal – 1 short.*

Turn to starboard to avoid any vessel forward of the beam where a risk of collision exists and you are the give-way vessel.

Power crossing situation

A power-driven vessel with another on its starboard side is the give-way vessel and should turn to starboard and pass astern of the other vessel.

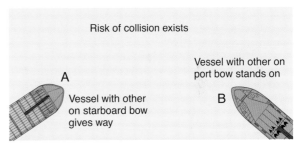

▲ *Both vessels under power and converging. A gives way to B. A to slow down or turn to starboard (1 short blast) and go astern of B.*

At night vessel A would see the port-side light of vessel B to starboard. Red for stop. The other vessel would see the green of the give-way vessel to port. Green for go.

A risk of collision should be established in plenty of time and action to avoid a collision should be taken early and the course alteration should be ample. Enough to show the stand-on vessel that you have given way. At night, show the other vessel a different aspect of your lights.

▲ *Two power-driven vessels, the oil tanker and the yacht raising its mainsail, and one sailing vessel.*

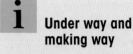

Under way and making way

- Under way – not at anchor, or made fast to the shore, or aground.
- Making way – propelled through the water by sail/machinery/oars.

▲ *A power-driven vessel (an air cushion vessel in non-displacement mode – hovercraft) going astern of us while we were under sail. Being a busy ferry service, they like to miss us – but not by much!*

? Closing with another vessel?

- Line up something on your boat with the other vessel; a stanchion is good.
- If the other vessel moves ahead of it, it is going ahead of you.
- If it moves astern of it, you are going ahead of it.
- If it remains lined up with the stanchion, you will collide.

Inshore, if the other vessel is chewing up the landscape and spitting it out astern, they are going ahead. If it is chewing up the landscape astern and spitting it out ahead, you are going ahead.

Fog

In fog:
- There are no stand-on or give-way vessels.
- It is everyone's responsibility to avoid a collision.
- If there are vessels moving in the vicinity, slow down to a minimum speed or stop. Head for shallow water if possible.
- Make sure you know the sound signals on the buoys. A number of buoys will have a sound fog signal. If you can identify them, although you can't see them, this will be a great help.

Keeping a lookout

Older chart plotters or chart plotters that are handling a number of overlays can take time for the screen to refresh and it can be quite a few seconds before you have all the data in front of you, certainly on vector charts.

It reminds us that keeping a lookout by all means is very important. This includes sight, sound, radar, AIS. In close quarters situations AIS is all very well, but for me you can't beat a keen eye, a pair of binoculars and a hand-bearing compass. Or, better still, a compass within the binoculars.

Narrow channels

You should stay outside narrow channels. You must not impede the passage of any vessel that needs to be in the narrow channel to navigate safely.

Traffic Separation Schemes (TSS)

Try to avoid these, but if it is necessary to cross a TSS then this must be done on a heading of 90° to the general direction of flow. You must not go down a TSS. They are for big ships only.

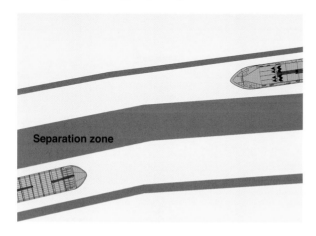

Radar

Radar is an extremely useful collision avoidance tool. But you do need to understand what you are looking at, whether you are viewing the relative bearing of you and another vessel or the true bearing.

AIS

An Automatic Identification System (AIS) is easy to understand and gives you an instant picture of the targets ahead, their SOG, COG, what they are and where they are bound.

Just for clarification, an AIS set that both transmits your data and receives data from others is called a 'transceiver' and not a 'transponder' as some say. A transponder is something that when interrogated responds with a signal. A RACON is a transponder, it recognises the sweep of your radar and this triggers it to respond with a signal which will appear on your radar screen. An active radar reflector is a transponder.

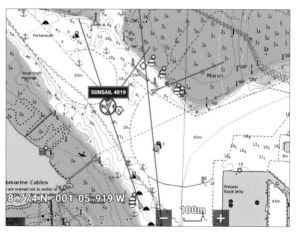

▲ AIS targets showing their COG – the blue line. Let's click on Sunsail 4019.

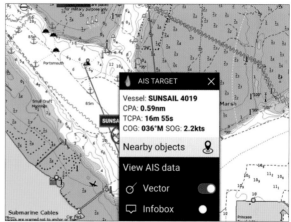

▲ The details for Sunsail 4019.

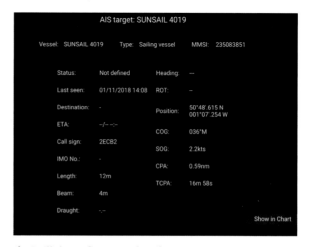

▲ Drill down for more details.

Vessel lights, day shapes and sound signals

In my view, regardless of whether you are at RYA Day Skipper level or Yachtmaster or the master of a VLCC, you need to know all the lights, day shapes and sound signals. I mean, what element of something lit up like a Christmas tree do you not want to understand? Knowing the tug and tow day shapes and lights could prevent you from heading straight between the two.

Vessel lights

Vessel lights can be sectored or all round.

Sectored lights for sidelights, port and starboard (red and green), for stern lights (white) and for steaming lights (white) are all taken to or from 22.5° abaft the beam.

This allows you to tell the aspect of a vessel.

All-round lights are used to identify certain aspects of what the vessel is doing and any restrictions or constraints it may be experiencing. They also let you know the order of priority in terms of stand-on or give-way at night.

Day shapes

Day shapes give us similar information:

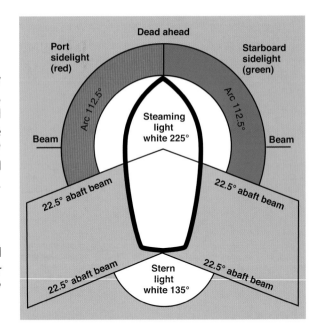

▲ Sectored lights.

▲ Power-driven over 50 metres in length.

▲ Restricted in ability to manoeuvre.

◄ Motoring cone telling you the sailboat is using its engine and thus a power-driven vessel.

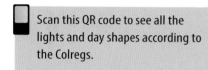

Scan this QR code to see all the lights and day shapes according to the Colregs.

Sound signals

Sound signals also tell you what a vessel is doing or is about to do.

A short sound signal is about one second and a long sound signal is four to six seconds.

Sound signals in sight of one another

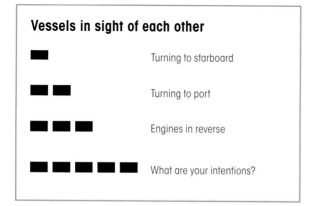

Vessels in sight of each other

Turning to starboard

Turning to port

Engines in reverse

What are your intentions?

There are also light signal versions of these sound signals to be made using an all-round white light:

- One flash — Turning to starboard
- Two flashes — Turning to port
- Three flashes — Running my engines astern
- Five flashes — What are your intentions?

Sound signals in narrow channels

Nearing a blind bend

I intend to overtake you on your starboard

I intend to overtake you on your port side

Affirmative

Negative

Sound signals in restricted visibility

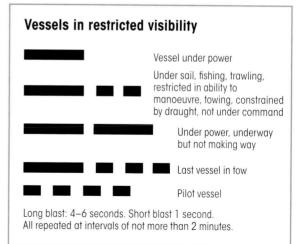

Vessels in restricted visibility

Vessel under power

Under sail, fishing, trawling, restricted in ability to manoeuvre, towing, constrained by draught, not under command

Under power, underway but not making way

Last vessel in tow

Pilot vessel

Long blast: 4–6 seconds. Short blast 1 second. All repeated at intervals of not more than 2 minutes.

Vessels in restricted visibility at anchor

Under 100m
– Rapid ringing of the bell for 5 seconds every minute.

Over 100m
– Rapid ringing of the bell 'forward' for 5 seconds, followed by rapid ringing of the gong 'aft' for 5 seconds every minute.

Vessels in restricted visibility aground

Under 100m
– 3 distinct strokes on the bell before and after the rapid ringing of the bell for 5 seconds every minute.

Over 100m
– 3 distinct strokes on the bell 'forward' before and after the rapid ringing of the bell for 5 seconds followed by rapid ringing of the gong 'aft' for 5 seconds every minute.

One other important day signal you see is the alpha flag, meaning 'I have a diver down, keep clear at low speed'.

▶ 'A' = Alpha flag

I have all the lights, shapes and signals for all the Colgregs on two sides of a card. They are reproduced here:

▼ *The Westview Sailing 'Lights, Shapes and Signals at a Glance' card – developed with Keith Bater.*

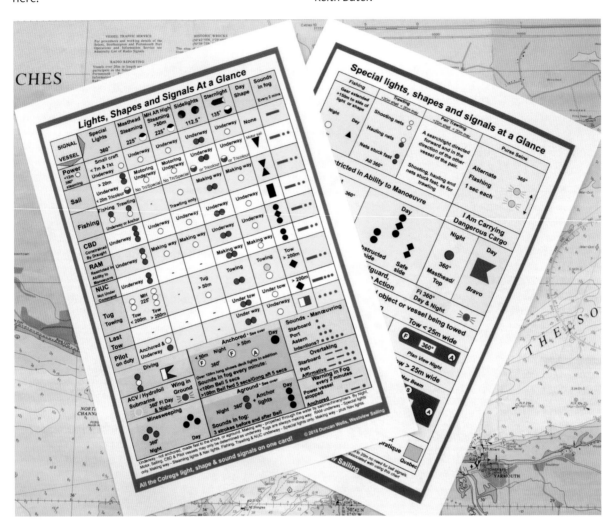

19 Weather

You don't set sail without a weather forecast. And you will get your forecast from the very sophisticated program on your phone, PC, tablet or chart plotter, which gives you wind strength and direction, and predictions.

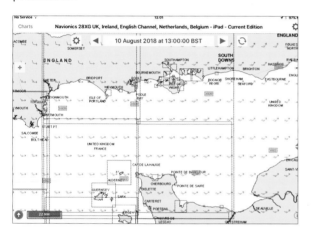

Most of the programs tend to give averages and can under-read wind strengths. That said, checking across a number of weather apps and becoming accustomed to what they are telling you is a wonderful, instant way of getting a very good idea of the weather.

Alternatively, you can work out the weather for yourself from the synoptic chart.

The sun heats the Earth, the air above the surface warms and rises and where that air rises, lifting a weight off the Earth, the pressure will be low. As the air rises through the atmosphere, it cools and falls back to Earth, increasing the weight on the Earth and causing high pressure.

So weather is measured in differences in pressure.

i Some general rules

- Warm air rises.
- Warm air rising takes weight off the ground and therefore reduces the pressure.
- Cold air falls.
- Cold air falling adds weight to the ground and increases the pressure.
- Warm air holds more water than cold air.
- Warm air cools as it rises.
- When it cools to a certain degree the water vapour in the air condenses out as cloud.

- When it cools even further this water vapour condenses out as droplets of rain or ice. The temperature at this point is called the dew point.
- Cold air moves faster than warm air.
- Wind wants to blow from high pressure to low pressure but is deflected by the Coriolis force and by friction from the ground. So the gradient wind blows nearly parallel to the isobars – at right angles to the pressure gradient.
- Wind direction is always described as where it is blowing FROM. So a north wind is blowing FROM the north.

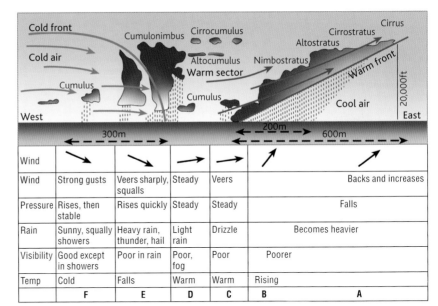

	F	E	D	C	B	A
Wind	↘	↘	→	→	↗	↗
Wind	Strong gusts	Veers sharply, squalls	Steady	Veers	Backs and increases	
Pressure	Rises, then stable	Rises quickly	Steady	Steady	Falls	
Rain	Sunny, squally showers	Heavy rain, thunder, hail	Light rain	Drizzle	Becomes heavier	
Visibility	Good except in showers	Poor in rain	Poor, fog	Poor	Poorer	
Temp	Cold	Falls	Warm	Warm	Rising	

▶ *The passage of a depression, a low, a cyclone.*

▼ *Synoptic chart with letters relating to the passage of a depression.*

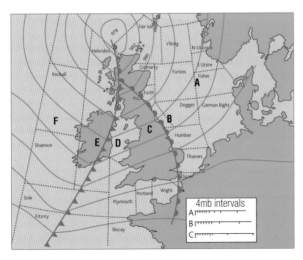

ℹ **Lapse rate**

The rate at which air cools as it rises is called the adiabatic lapse rate. Dry air cools at 10°C every 1,000m it rises. Moist or saturated air cools at the rate of 5.5°C every 1,000m it rises.

Dry air is air that contains its moisture content invisibly.

Saturated air is air where the moisture content has condensed out as fog or rain.

Scenarios

Sunny day

This is a result of cold air falling, high pressure. Cold air falling, the skies are clear and the sun is able to warm up the ground and you have a warm sunny day. At night it will cool quickly and you will notice the coolness of the cold air falling.

Cloudy, rainy day

This is a result of warm moist air rising, low pressure. Warm moist air rises and cools. The vapour condenses out as cloud. If it cools further, droplets of rain are

▲ *Sunny day, cold air falling.*

▲ *Warm air rising and condensing out as cloud and rain.*

▲ *Cloud on a sunny day.*

formed or perhaps ice. At night, being overcast the ground is unable to radiate its heat as it would if the sky had been clear and being overcast you have warm air rising so the night air is not so cold.

Cloud on a sunny day

The sun has warmed the ground, a parcel of warm moist air has risen and cooled and condensed out as cloud.

What the clouds mean

Cirrus cloud

The highest level of cloud, which has been beaten up by a great deal of wind and is wispy. The wispy effect is the ice crystals – it is very high in the sky and therefore very cold up there – that have been blown to smithereens by this strong wind. Cirrus invariably tells you that a depression is on the way.

▲ *Cirrus.*

Cumulus cloud

The fluffy cumulus cloud is caused by the sun warming up the ground and the air above it rising (warm air rises) and, as it rises, cooling. The water vapour in the air then condenses out as cloud – cumulus cloud. A cumulus cloud would be associated with high pressure, cold air falling, cold air that has been warmed as a result of the sun beating down on the Earth, which has caused this cold air to warm up and rise and the vapour within it to condense out as cumulus cloud.

Stratus

Stratus clouds are low-level, layered clouds. They are created when a light wind blows warmer moist air over a colder surface. Where cirrus and cumulus clouds are individual and distinct, separate clouds, stratus is general, a covering, a layer.

Nimbus

Means rainy. A nimbus cloud will be grey and contains rain. You will need an umbrella if you stand under a nimbus cloud. Nimbus is often general and layered and is referred to as nimbostratus. Nimbus cloud will be associated with low pressure, warm air rising and condensing out as cloud and rain.

Cumulonimbus

This is the storm cloud that you find before a cold front. It is a system of its very own, with warm air rising up inside and cold air falling down at the sides. Aeroplanes will want to avoid this type of cloud as the updraught and downdraught can rip wings off. A cumulonimbus cloud will give you thunder and lightning.

Frontal systems

A low-pressure system (cyclone/depression), warm air rising, has winds rushing into it, converging.

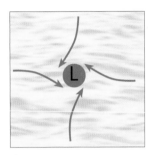 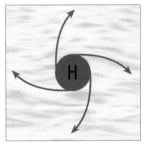

▲ *A low: warm air rising, winds converge.*

▲ *A high: cold air falling, winds diverge.*

A high-pressure system (anticyclone), cold air falling, has winds rushing out of it, diverging.

The key to forecasting the weather is to look at the synoptic charts, to look at the sky and to monitor the pressure. And to keep doing this until you can match up what you are seeing with what the synoptic charts are telling you.

Halo round the moon or sun?

This is caused by cirrus cloud high above you and its ice crystals. You are having a lovely day or evening, but a depression is on the way. The halo effect is the light refracting through the crystals.

Coriolis force

Why do winds blow anticlockwise round a low in the northern hemisphere and clockwise in the southern hemisphere?

Because of the Coriolis force.

Scan this QR code to watch a graphic description of the Coriolis force in action.

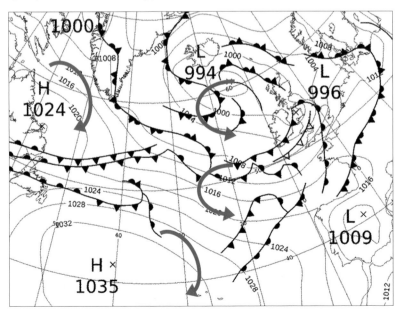

Isobars

Close together: windy and rainy
Further apart: less wind and sunshine

Even during the passage of a depression, there will be areas with sunshine and less wind; just look for a widening of the isobars.

◀ *Wind blows anticlockwise round a low and clockwise round a high in the northern hemisphere and the opposite – clockwise round a low and anticlockwise round a high – in the southern hemisphere.*

Wind does not follow the direction of the isobar exactly, but is backed a little off it. You can measure the speed of the wind by measuring the distance between two isobars and taking it to the scale. Find your latitude and read off the wind speed in knots.

Occluded fronts

Cold air moves faster than warm air – warm air has more water in it and moves more slowly. So when the cold front catches up with the warm front, the front becomes occluded. This is shown as a zipping up between the warm-front semicircles and the cold-front spikes.

There is cold air ahead of the warm front and the cold front behind is squeezing this warm air up. As it does, it condenses out as cloud and when the dew point is reached, it rains. There are two types of occluded front: a warm one where the cold air ahead of the warm front is warmer than the cold air behind it; and a cold one where the cold air ahead of the warm front is colder than the cold air behind it. Either way it will be raining.

Buys Ballot's Law

With your back to the wind the low will be on your left (in the northern hemisphere), the high will therefore be to your right. In the southern hemisphere this is reversed.

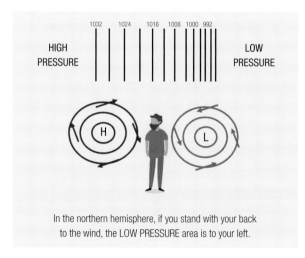

In the northern hemisphere, if you stand with your back to the wind, the LOW PRESSURE area is to your left.

▲ Buys Ballot's law.

Weather effects on wind direction (northern hemisphere)	
Warm front	Wind backs before the front and then veers as it goes through and strengthens
Mid front	Wind direction stays steady
Cold front	As the front goes through, the wind veers sharply
Occluded fronts	Wind veers as the front goes through
Land and sea	Wind backs as a result of friction by 15° when it blows over sea. Wind backs as a result of friction by 30° when it blows over land.
Converging wind	Wind blowing parallel to a coastline where the sea is to the left of the land will be stronger – the wind on the land is backed by 30° and the wind over the sea is backed by 15°, so they are converging
Diverging wind	Wind blowing parallel to a coastline where the sea is to the right of the land will be weaker – the wind on the sea is backed by 15° and the wind on the land is backed by 30°, so the two are diverging.

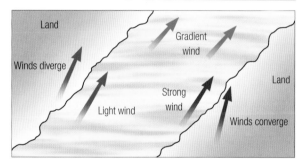

▲ Converging and diverging winds.

Jet stream

In the UK, if the jet stream is:

- to the north of us, it will drag warm Mediterranean air up. We will have warmer than average weather.
- to the south of us, it will bring cold polar air down. We will have colder than average weather.
- directly above us, it will increase the severity of any depression as it sucks warm air upwards, resulting in windier and wetter weather.

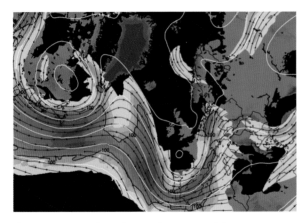

▲ Jet stream below the UK dragging cold air over us.

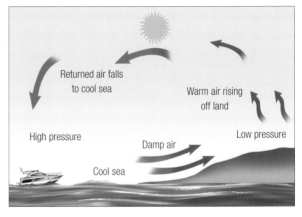

▲ Sea breeze.

Sea breeze

Land heats up and cools down more quickly than water. The sun heats the land. The air rises, resulting in low pressure on the land. Colder air from the sea, which is at a higher pressure than the rising air from the land, blows towards the land. The rising warm air moves out to sea and cools and, as it falls, creates high pressure over the sea.

This cycle continues until the heat source stops – the sun sets.

Land breeze

When the sun sets, the land cools quickly. The sea is now warmer than the land and the cyle is reversed.

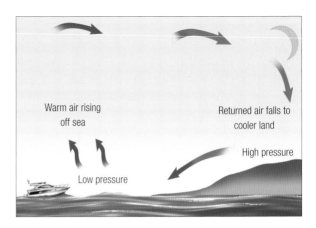

▲ Land breeze.

Crossed winds rule

If you stand with your back to the wind in the northern hemisphere* and the upper wind – or rather the clouds – moves across you from left to right, then the weather will deteriorate. You are in front of the depression or low.

If you stand with your back to the wind and the upper wind (or clouds) comes from right to left, the weather will improve. You are at the back of, or behind, the low.

*In the southern hemisphere you stand facing the wind.

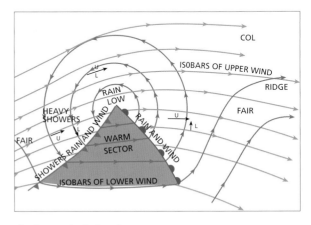

▲ Crossed winds rule.

Backing and veering

The direction from which the forecast wind is blowing is called the 'initial wind'. Say this is north. If the wind direction changes and moves anticlockwise round the compass and starts blowing from the north-west it, is described as backing. If it moves clockwise round the compass and starts blowing from the north-east, it is described as veering.

Wind over tide

Wind blowing in the opposite direction to the set of the tide will create short steep seas.

Wind blowing in the same direction as the set of the tide will flatten the sea out.

Wind and water

When the wind blows over the water, it piles the water up into wavelets and then waves. And the greater the distance of the stretch of water – the fetch – that the wind is able to blow, the bigger the waves. If at the same time the seabed is shelving and the depth of water is reducing (which encourages the waves to break, as happens on a beach), then the wind blowing over this will have an even greater effect and will pile the waves higher. The Bay of Biscay is an example of this.

On a calm day you can tell where the puffs of wind are because you see a darkened patch of water where the wind has made little wavelets. The direction of the wind is always at 90° to the line of the wavelets.

▲ Direction of wind according to wavelets.

Shipping forecast

In the UK the Coastguard gives the inshore shipping forecast every three hours. It announces this Maritime Safety Information Broadcast, including a weather forecast, on VHF Channel 16 and advises on which working channel it will be broadcast.

Key terminology		
Timing	Imminent	Within 6 hours*
	Soon	Between 6 and 12 hours*
	Later	Between 12 and 24 hours*
Wind strength	Given according to the Beaufort scale, which ranges from 0 (calm) to 12 (hurricane). Gale force is 8.	
Sea state	Smooth, Slight, Moderate, Rough, Very Rough	
Weather	Mist, Fog, Showers, Rain, Fair	
Visibility	Good	More than 5 nautical miles
	Moderate	2–5 nautical miles
	Poor	1,000 metres to 2 nautical miles
	Very poor	Less than 1,000 metres
Pressure**	Steady	Less than 0.1mb
	Rising/falling slowly	0.1–1.5mb
	Rising/falling	1.6–3.5mb
	Rising/falling quickly	3.6–6.0mb
	Rising/falling very rapidly	More than 6.0mb

*This not from the time the forecast was prepared or from when you are hearing it, but from the start time of the period of the forecast.

**Pressure tendencies are measured over three-hour periods. A big change such as 6mb in three hours will give you a strong wind – Force 6 on the Beaufort scale.

Fog

Caused by warm air over a cold surface.

Advection Fog: warm air over a cold sea – dispersed by wind

Radiation Fog: warm air over cold land – dispersed by the sun

The Beaufort scale

Force 1	Light Airs	1–3 knots
Force 2	Light Breeze	4–6 knots
Force 3	Gentle Breeze	7–10 knots
Force 4	Moderate Breeze	11–16 knots
Force 5	Fresh Breeze	17–21 knots
Force 6	Strong Breeze	22–27 knots
Force 7	Near Gale	28–33 knots
Force 8	Gale	34–40 knots
Force 9	Severe Gale	41–47 knots
Force 10	Storm	45–55 knots
Force 11	Violent Storm	56–63 knots
Force 12	Hurricane Force	>64 knots

i **Glossary**

- Isobar – line of equal pressure
- Gradient wind – the predicted wind
- Filling – a front is reducing/disappearing, the weather will get better
- Deepening – the pressure difference at the front is increasing, the weather will get worse.

20 Pilotage

Pilotage is a matter of using what you can see around you and working with that to navigate safely. Pilotage is what you do when inshore. Passage making is what you do when offshore.

Key concepts

Identifying buoys

Make sure you are looking at the correct buoy. At night, make sure you watch a light run through a couple of sequences so you know the characteristic and can identify the light on the chart or chart plotter.

Transits

Transits are an instant visual way of checking where you are and knowing where you are going.

▲ When these two chimneys go out of transit you can cross safely over the mud bank.

▼ Showing that the bearing of your transit by eye and on chart matched with the chart plotter. You are somewhere down this 273°T line.

USING TWO HEADLANDS AS A TRANSIT

Headlands nearly in transit

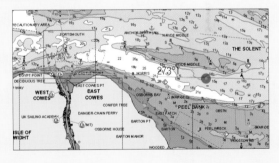

Headlands in transit

273°T

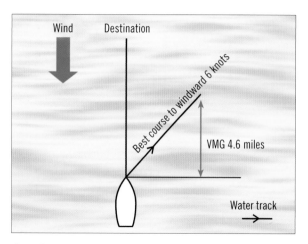

▲ Velocity made good.

Velocity made good

This is just progress towards your destination when you are having to tack your way there.

Tacking up the cone

When making for a destination you can be sure that the wind, whatever it was doing before, will now start to blow from where you are aiming for and so you will need to tack.

Draw out a cone 15° either side of the destination and tack down that.

Clearing bearings

Set yourself clearing bearings down the cone and tack when you reach them.

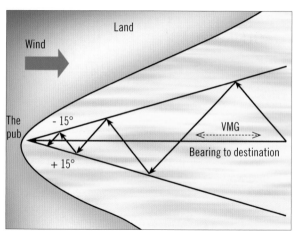

▲ Tack when you reach the clearing bearings.

Check if there are dangers near where you aim to sail and adjust the clearing bearings accordingly.

Head bearings

If you have taken a head bearing on a charted mark, make a note on your matt laminated sheet of the head bearing and what to do if the bearing increases or decreases.

Back bearings

Do the same for back bearings. It can be confusing working out which way to turn when the back bearing changes.

Draw a picture of what you are about to do.

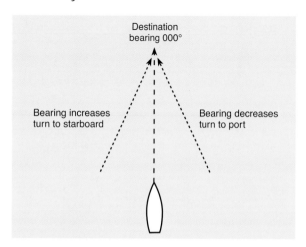

▲ Head bearings.

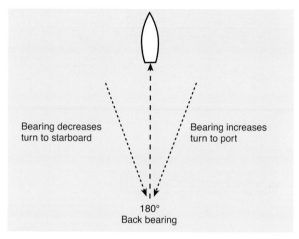

▲ Back bearings.

'ROLLING ROAD'

The 'Rolling Road' mentioned in Colin Jarman, Garth Cooper and Dick Holness's *East Coast Pilot* is an excellent idea.

It doesn't need to be hugely detailed, but you do need to know the bearing and distance from one mark to another and the exact appearance or light sequence of each mark, so you can tick them off as you pass them.

Here you are going to enter Southsea Marina in Langstone Harbour. The route turns over 180° on itself.

Start next to the Q.R (quick red) port-hand marker at the entrance to Langstone Harbour in position 50°47'.2N by 001°01'.6W.

▶ The chartlet shows you the buoys you must pass.

▶ The 'Rolling Road' simply takes this information and puts it on to a piece of paper that you can follow, with courses, distances, the direction to turn and the buoys you will pass.

Magnetic variation is just 1°W so I have ignored it for the purposes of the exercise.

▶ Or more neatly.

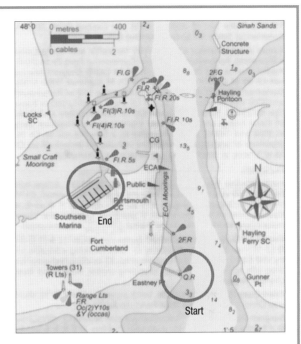

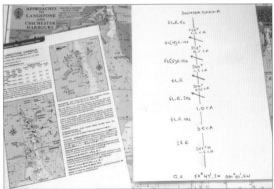

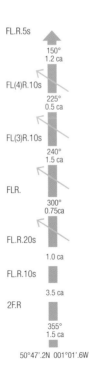

Of course, you could do this on the chart plotter with Dock to Dock.

It's a good idea to interrogate each lateral mark before you set off so you know what to look for and don't go past one mark until you have identified the next. Avoid entering an unfamiliar harbour at night. Stand off, heave to or anchor until daylight.

Involve the crew. Let them know what the plan is and give everyone a job. Have someone on the hand-bearing compass reading out bearings, someone on the depth sounder, someone on lookout.

21 Passage planning

Chart plotters can do all the routing work for you. Some will offer you the chance of great circle routes or rhumb line routes. Many of them will give you a course to steer allowing for the tides. Some will suggest the best time to make the passage. You can set wave height limits and wind strength limits to make the passage as comfortable as possible.

But you can also do it yourself on a paper chart. Passage planning is a matter of getting from your start position to your destination as efficiently and safely as possible, and as enjoyably as possible.

It's about using the tide to your advantage. Believe me, it is no fun stemming a four-knot tide when you are doing six knots through the water. You will only be making two knots over the ground. Much better to be going with the tide and doing ten knots over the ground.

Considerations for passage planning

1. Are there any restrictions about departing? Do you have to negotiate a lock, or wait for enough water to get over a sill, or get off a mud berth?

2. Are there any restrictions about your destination – a sill to get over?

3. Are there any tidal gates that you need to make? A tidal gate being a time by which you need to be in a particular place to take advantage of the tide. The

▲ *Chart plotters indicating route, bearing and distance between waypoints, course to steer, time taken.*

▲ *Arriving at a harbour with a sill? When can you gain access?*

Alderney Race is an example. Arrive at the top of the race at HW Dover and you will be swept down the race by the tide. Miss this timing and you could be facing as much as seven knots of tide against you. For me sailing at six knots, that means going backwards at one knot. Not awfully funny.

4. Check for boltholes along the way, safe harbours that you could head for if conditions became too much.

5. Decide what conditions might be too much for your boat and, more importantly, your crew.

6. Get a weather forecast for the duration of the passage.

7. Consider the effect of wind over tide – wind against tide will shorten the sea and could make it uncomfortable. The greater the 'fetch', the distance that wind has been able to blow over the water, the more the sea will have built up. Wind generally doesn't hurt a boat, but waves do and it is the wind that creates the waves.

8. Provision correctly. This includes fuel and water.

9. Bad weather. I would argue that with coastal passages bad weather can be avoided by delaying the voyage. There is nothing wrong with being stormbound in port. Navigation needs to be planned in advance. The boat has to be set with reefed sails, warm clothes for everyone, wet weather gear, life jackets, lifelines, the boat stowed for sea, hatches battened down, sandwiches made in readiness, soup in flasks (no one will want to go below if there is a lot of movement to the boat).

10. Fog

If fog closes in:
- Establish your position before the fog reaches you.
- Engine on, sail down.
- All hands on deck.
- Life jackets on for everyone.
- Navigation lights and steaming light on.
- VHF radio on, large vessels often tell the coast-guard what visibility they have and where they are.
- Radar on.
- Make the appropriate fog sound signal.
- Head for shallow water.

 Navigating at night

The beauty of navigating at night is that the whole world comes to life, or should I say to light. Everything is so much clearer. That smudge off to starboard by day becomes the quick flashing green mark by night. As clear as day, clearer. The container ship on your port side, which in open waters whether you are sailing or motoring should give way to you, can be seen at night clearly altering course when its high white steaming light aft comes into line with its low white steaming light forward and you know they are going astern of you. It's much harder to see this by day – unless you have an AIS, of course.

 Handy tip: Warm drinks

Do not make drinks, soup, tea or coffee too hot. If the drink comes out of the flask piping hot, no one can drink it. The idea of a warming drink is just that. I want it now and hot enough but not burning. Too hot and I will have to let it cool. In a thermos mug this could take weeks, in an ordinary mug it will probably spill before it is cool enough.

Scan the QR code to watch a video of a passage plan from the Hamble to Jersey.

22 Anchoring

The key to anchoring is having good ground tackle, adhering to the 'Five Essentials of Anchoring' and knowing exactly how much cable (chain or rope) you have let out.

Anchor options				
Type	**Make**	**For**	**Against**	**Bottom**
Fisherman	Fisherman	Folds flat. Good on rock and kelp	Poor power to weight ratio	Rock/kelp
Plough	CQR/Plough	Good all rounder. The hinged shank is designed to avoid tripping with the turn of the tide	The hinged shank doesn't always prevent it tripping with the turn of the tide, but it usually resets itself	All types, use a tripping line if anchoring on rock
	Delta	Strong, sets quickly, self launching		All types, use a tripping line for rock
	Kobra	Strong, sets quickly, self launching		All types, use a tripping line for rock
Claw	Bruce	Strong		All types, use a tripping line for rock
Light weight	Danforth – Steel Fortress – Aluminium Brittany	Stows flat. Can vary the angle of the flukes to match harder or softer seabeds	Can be hard to set in harder seabeds. Can trip and then not reset. Best used as a kedge anchor	Clay, sand and mud
Modern	Spade	Strong, sets quickly, self launching		All types, use a tripping line for rock
	Rocna	Strong, sets very quickly, self launching	Check the quality of the steel, some were made with inferior steel	All types, use a tripping line for rock
	Manson Supreme	Strong, sets very quickly, clever self-tripping slot, self launching		All types, use a tripping line for rock
	Ultra	Strong, sets very quickly, self righting, self launching		All types, use a tripping line for rock
	Bugel	Strong, sets very quickly, self righting		All types, use a tripping line for rock
Grapnel	Grapnel	Folds up, used for light work	Used as a kedge anchor or for dinghies	Anything really

Ground tackle

You need ground tackle that is man enough for the job, an anchor and chain or a chain/rope combination that are the correct specification for the boat.

▲ CQR or plough.

▲ Delta.

▲ Bruce secured on a lanyard.

▲ Fortress (aluminium), Danforth are made of steel.

▲ Grapnel on 10m chain, then warp.

▲ Rocna secured with a drop nose pin.

▲ Ultra.

Five essentials of anchoring

Shelter	Not a lee shore, or likely to become one, no nasty tides.
Not prohibited	Not a fairway, not a shipping lane, not restricted/prohibited.
Depth	Enough depth at LW and enough chain/warp at HW.
Holding	Will the bottom give good holding for your type of anchor? Mud and sand are good, rock not always so good.
Swinging	Is there room to swing when the tide turns, or if you are to get blown about by the breeze?

> ### ℹ Kedge anchor
>
> A kedge anchor is a second anchor, with the bower anchor (the anchor on the bow) being your primary anchor. The kedge anchor is so called because if you were to run aground on a sandbank, then you would row an anchor out in the dinghy, set it and then 'kedge' the boat off the sandbank. A kedge anchor can be any type of anchor, but they are often the Danforth or Fortress type.

Alphabetical colour code									
	5m	10m	15m	20m	25m	30m	35m	40m	45m
English	Black	Blue	Brown	Green	Pink	Red	Yellow	2 × Black	2 × Blue
French	Bleu	Brun	Jaune	Noir	Rose	Rouge	Vert	2 × Bleu	2 × Brun
German	Blau	Braun	Gelb	Grün	Rosa	Rot	Schwarz	2 × Blau	2 × Braun
Welsh	Coch	Du	Glas	Glyrrd	Gwrm	Melyn	Pinc	2 × Coch	2 × Du

◀ *All chain. Silks tied to the links.*

▲ *For those to whom snooker means nothing, simply take the same colours and run them alphabetically.*

Coding the cable

The key to successful anchoring is paying out enough cable. To know how much you are paying out, you need to mark the cable with a code you can readily understand.

Snooker

For some reason I seem to be able to remember the order in which one pots the snooker balls, despite not playing the game.

And so I mark my chain with coloured silks tied in at five-metre intervals in the order that one pots the snooker balls: red, yellow, green, brown, blue, pink, black. And because that only gets me to 35 metres and my chain is 50 metres in length, go back to the beginning and double up, so:

1 × Red	=	5m
1 × Yellow	=	10m
1 × Green	=	15m
1 × Brown	=	20m
1 × Blue	=	25m
1 × Pink	=	30m
1 × Black	=	35m
2 × Red	=	40m
2 × Yellow	=	45m

Place the anchor on the dock and pull out all the chain from the anchor locker and with a tape measure off the five-metre intervals.

Now if I see a piece of pink silk flying above the water I know I have 30 metres of cable out. And this I can remember even after a serious session in the pub.

If the cable is mainly rope, or warp as it's called, you will have ten metres of chain between the anchor and the warp, to help the anchor dig in and set. You can tie the silks into the strands, whether it be three-strand or multiplait, or bind coloured cotton around.

It is also important to put this code inside a foredeck locker lid so that new crew know what it all means.

I call these silks Anchor Buddies and you can order them from westviewsailing.co.uk.

How much scope to allow

- a minimum of 4 × depth for chain.
- a minimum of 6 × depth for warp.

When calculating depth, don't forget to allow for the distance from bow roller to water.

And if the wind is likely to pipe up, veer a little extra cable, assuming you have room in the anchorage.

Chain in the anchor locker does no good at all so you might as well pay it out, as long as you have room.

Quick tips for anchoring success

Setting the anchor

Anchor into the tide, unless the strength of the wind is greater than the tide.

In tidal waters, the pull of the boat as it is dragged

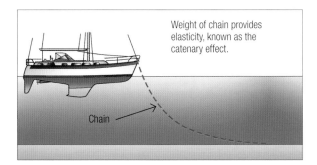

Weight of chain provides elasticity, known as the catenary effect.

Chain

▲ *Scope chain.*

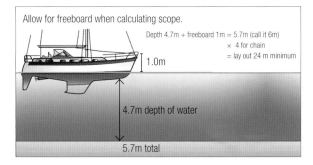

To provide elasticity we need much more warp than chain. Plus 10 metres of chain between anchor and warp.

Warp

Chain

▲ *Scope warp.*

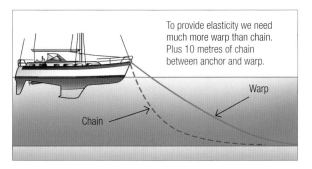

Allow for freeboard when calculating scope.

Depth 4.7m + freeboard 1m = 5.7m (call it 6m)
× 4 for chain
= lay out 24 m minimum

1.0m

4.7m depth of water

5.7m total

▲ *Scope allowing for freeboard.*

▲ *Holding to a snubber.*

▲ *A stopper to prevent the chain running out.*

back by the tide should get the anchor to set. In non-tidal waters, or at slack water, backing up to set the anchor will help.

Snatching?

If the boat is snatching at the anchor, in a bit of a chop, then veer more cable. Or add a rope snubber to the chain with a rolling hitch and then back on board to a cleat. Once secure, veer more chain so the boat is holding to the snubber and chain. I always use a snubber, so the strain is taken on the cleat rather than my expensive windlass.

? What's a cable?

The length of anchor warp on ships of the line was 100 fathoms or 600 feet, which equates to 182.88 metres. There being 1,852 metres in a nautical mile, 182.88 metres is one-tenth of a mile (well, close enough). So a 'cable' is also one-tenth of a nautical mile.

How to tell if your anchor is holding

1. Place your hand outside the bow roller on to the cable. If it is quiet you are holding. If it is vibrating you may be on the move.

2. Fix something on shore and monitor this by eye or bearing.

3. Set an anchor alarm on the GPS.

Preventing the cable from jumping off the bow roller

If the anchorage is a bit lively and you haven't set a snubber, there is the chance that the anchor cable might jump off the bow roller. To stop this from happening, add in a split pin or a lashing between the bow roller cheeks.

Securing the anchor on board

You don't want the anchor jumping out of its mount and setting itself unexpectedly, so attach it to the boat. A lashing will do, or a lanyard. Often bow cheeks have a split pin for securing the anchor.

Never shackle the anchor chain to the boat

Always attach the bitter end of the anchor chain to the boat with a lashing or length of rope so you can cut it quickly if you need to free yourself from the anchor in a hurry.

▲ *Lash or tie the anchor to the boat.*

Hoop to stop the chain from jumping off the bow roller

▲ *Some bow cheeks have a hoop between the two to prevent the cable from jumping out.*

▲ *Here, a lashing holds the anchor in place.*

Displaying the correct signal

The anchor signal by day is one black ball where it can best be seen in the 'forepart of the vessel'. At night you show an all-round white light where it can best be seen.

Swinging room

Look at how the other boats in the anchorage are lying. Heavy displacement sailing boats will lie to the tide rather than the wind. Flybridge motorboats with medium or deep V hulls will lie more to the wind than the tide. Choose your spot carefully.

What happens when the tide turns?

Anchors that bury themselves into the seabed will generally handle the turn of the tide without tripping. If they do trip, you want them to set themselves again quickly. Danforths and Fortress anchors can be hard to reset. The modern breed of Rocna, Manson and Bugel anchors will reset themselves very quickly. Delta, Spade and CQR anchors should also reset themselves.

Anchor stuck?

If you can't get the anchor up because it's caught on something, try driving the boat over the anchor. Try working the boat around and lifting the anchor from different angles. If it really won't come up then you will need to leave the anchor (at least £500) and the chain (again, at least £500) behind. As no one wants to lose £1,000 it is worth buoying the chain, marking the spot with the MOB function on the GPS plotter and hoping that the local dive company will look kindly on you.

Tripping eye

You could, of course, attach a tripping line to the eyelet in the crown of the anchor, or the bar of a Rocna, Manson, Bugel, which will allow you to pull the anchor out backwards, if it gets stuck. To set this up in advance suggests that you are not confident of the bottom and if that was the case I would do my best to avoid anchoring there. If I had to anchor in an emergency I might set a tripping line as a precaution. I already have an emergency – I don't need another emergency when I find I can't get my anchor out.

▲ Anchor chain with buoy attached, ready to throw in.

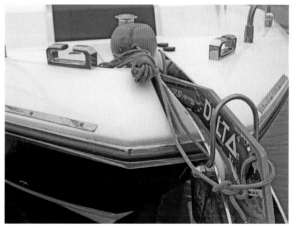

▲ Attached to the tripping eye and ready to deploy.

◀ Tripping line and buoy.

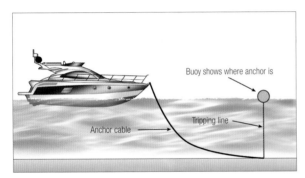

▲ *Tripping line and buoy set.*

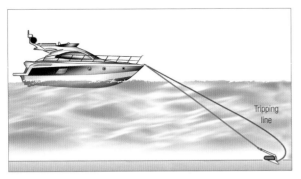

▲ *Anchor caught under a cable.*

▲ *Using tripping line to free it.*

▲ *Anchor free.*

 Glossary

- Cable – Anchor chain or warp or chain/warp combination (British English)
- Capstan – Vertically mounted motor for lowering and raising the anchor
- Devil's claw – Mechanical break to stop the chain paying out
- Ground tackle – Anchor and chain, or anchor and warp or anchor and warp/chain combination
- Gypsy – Wheel on the windlass with teeth to engage the chain
- Lee shore – Shore on to which the wind is blowing. Don't anchor on a lee shore because if your anchor were to drag and you could not start the engine then you would be blown on to the shore and shipwrecked.
- Rode – Anchor chain or warp or chain/warp combination (American English)
- Scope – Amount of cable or rode you have veered/let out
- Snubber – Short line from the cable/rode to a cleat on board to prevent snatching or jerking and to take the strain off a windlass.
- Veer – Let out or pay out
- Warp – Rope used for anchoring or mooring
- Weather shore – A shore from which the wind is blowing. If you anchor on a weather shore and your anchor drags and you are unable to start your engine, you will at least be blown out to sea.
- Windlass – Horizontally mounted motor for lowering and raising the anchor.

 Scan the QR code to watching a video on anchoring.

23 Safety

Navigation is not just the matter of departing from one point and arriving at another, but departing from one point and arriving safely at another. And it is the responsibility of the skipper to show the crew how to handle an emergency safely.

Safety equipment is expensive and if you ever need to use it you want to know that it is going to work. So you need to look after it.

Don't leave lifebuoys and their lights or Danbuoys on the back rail, store them inside the boat when not at sea. That way, batteries and bulbs will survive and the dreaded UV won't attack your gear. Check the bulb cover on the lifebuoy light, it is a favourite place for gathering water. I also remove the batteries from the lifebuoy lights so they don't corrode while I am not looking. I put them into the lights and check them only when at sea and it is dark enough to need the lights.

Safety equipment

Life jackets

Life jackets need to be serviced annually. Ideally send these to a life jacket service centre, but if you are going to do the service yourself, check that:

- The firing head is in date.
- The cylinder is in good condition, has not been fired and weighs what it says on the side.

Inflate the life jacket and check that the bladder is in good condition with no holes. Wipe it down to remove salt and sand and dry in the airing cupboard inflated for 24 hours. Then pack according to manufacturer's instructions.

Check that other kit (personal locator/AIS beacons, light, spray hood, MOB Lifesaver) are in good condition and in date. My favourite beacon is

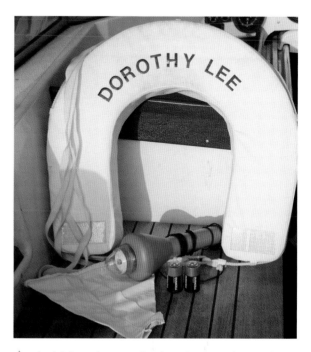

▲ This lifebuoy lives inside when I'm not sailing and is ten years old.

the Ocean Signal MOB1 DSC/AIS, which needs to be fitted by an approved retailer or service centre. The MOB1 sends a DSC VHF call to the mother ship and then sends its position out on AIS.

Added to which, a life jacket for me must have a sprayhood and light, as well as crotch straps and an MOB Lifesaver.

Flares

Flares need to be kept in a canister or, better still, in a nice padded attaché case, which not only keeps them dry but stops them rattling about. And you need to check that they are in date. It's worth having a maintenance notebook with a list of all the expiry and service dates, so you don't forget.

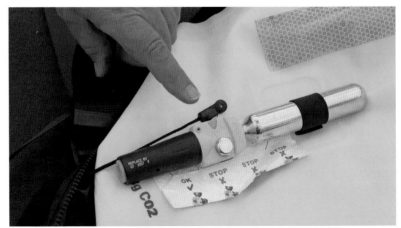

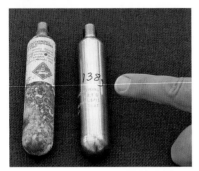

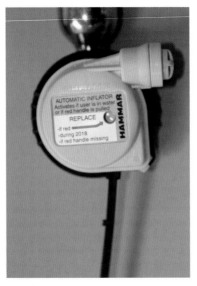

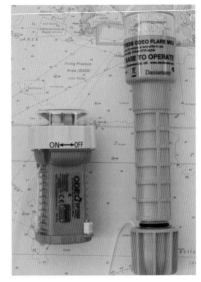

Liferafts

Liferafts needs to be serviced by a professional safety company. I no longer own a liferaft as it is cheaper to rent. Also, I used to have a six-man liferaft but only ever sailed with a maximum of two peple. I now rent a four-man. The saving is worth thinking about.

Fire extinguishers

Fire extinguishers should be serviced annually and they do have expiry dates, check these.

i Walk the boat

Safety isn't just about the equipment available to help you get out of trouble. Making sure you don't get into trouble in the first place is the best policy. So let's check the boat and the systems and make sure that they are not likely to fail. All pilots 'walk the plane' before flying and you should do the same – 'walk the boat'.

▲ Jackstay shackle moused to a deck point.

▲ Guard wire lashed to guardrail can be dropped in a hurry if this is what you want.

▲ Jackstay is lashed aft to a deck point.

Jackstays

Check for chafing and wear. Check the anchor points forward and aft. Jackstays should be attached by a moused shackle forward and a lashing aft so they can be cut away quickly in an emergency.

Guardrails

It's up to you. I don't need to drop the guardrails as I will bring the MOB in over the upper guard wire and I like the security of having the upper guard wire in place when I am working about the deck. But if you want to be able to lose the guard wires in a hurry then they need to be secured at one end with a lashing.

Lifelines and harnesses

Check the strapping for wear and chafe. Check that the carabiners close properly.

Engines and outboards

Engines and outboards need annual servicing.
Inboard engines need a daily 'WOBBLE':

W Water – Fresh water, check the header tank
O Oil – Engine oil check, periodically check the gearbox oil
B Belt – Alternator belt looks OK? Tension OK? Half an inch of play?
B Battery – Battery topped up? Terminals OK?
L Leaks – Any nasty leaks under the engine?
E Exhaust – Water coming out of the exhaust when the engine is running?

Note: If you are going to take the lid or top off the raw water filter to check the strainer, make sure that the O-Ring in the top, the seal, doesn't fall out. Screwing the lid back on without the seal in place allows air to be sucked in, no raw water will enter your cooling system and the engine will overheat. It's the number one cause of overheated engines, so I am told.

Raising the alarm

If a person or ship are in grave and imminent danger and require immediate assistance, call a Mayday (after the French for help me, m'aidez) and send a digital Distress Alert on the DSC VHF radio, followed up by a voice call on VHF Channel 16, or send a distress alert via an Emergency Position Indicating Radio Beacon (EPIRB), Personal Locator Beacon (PLB) or certain AIS beacons.

There are a number of other ways of signalling a distress:

- SOS by any means, light, sound Morse: 'dit dit dit, dah dah dah, dit dit dit'
- Pyrotechnic red rocket flares
- Pyrotechnic red handheld flares
- Pyrotechnic orange smoke flares, handheld or a canister on the water
- Flying a ball over a square
- Flying the signal flags 'No' over 'Yes'
- Flames on the vessel (as from a burning tar barrel, oil barrel etc)
- Waving the arms up and down
- A noise by any means, rapid firing of a gun, a horn, banging sounds

Use whatever distress alert makes sense for you at the time, although I think you should avoid the 'burning tar barrel'.

The first 15 minutes of any rescue make all the difference so whether you are fully crewed or on your own you need to alert the Coastguard as soon as you can. With your position, they can get someone to come out to you.

- Hit the Distress Alert on the VHF/DSC radio.
- Follow up with a voice call on Channel 16.

If you follow the acronym MIRPDANIO you will be able to get over, in 90 seconds, all the information to allow the rescuers to mount the fastest, most effective rescue.

MIRPDANIO

Here Yacht *Fairwind* (call sign of GION6 and MMSI No 235086183 in position 50°47'.2N by 001°17'.5W) has hit a submerged object and is holed and sinking. There are five persons on board. They will have to take to the liferaft in ten minutes.

Here's how the MIRPDANIO acronym goes, as follows:

Letter	Explanation	You say:
M	is for Mayday	Mayday, Mayday, Mayday.
I	is for Identify yourself	This is Yacht *Fairwind*, *Fairwind*, *Fairwind*, MMSI No 235086183 Call Sign Golf India Oscar November Six.

(Slight pause to allow everyone who is listening to get a pencil and paper to write down the details)

Letter	Explanation	You say:
R	is for Repeat this information	Mayday, this is Yacht *Fairwind*. MMSI No 235086183. Call sign Golf India Oscar November Six.
P	is for Position	We are in position 50°47'.2N by 001°17'.5W.
D	is for Distress	We are holed and sinking.
A	is for Assistance required	We require immediate assistance.
N	is for Number on board	There are five persons on board.
I	is for any other Information	We will be taking to the liferaft in ten minutes.
O	is for Over	Over.

If you are not in grave and imminent danger but want to alert the coastguard to an issue (say there is a problem with your rudder, you are several miles off the coast and not in danger at present and are trying to fix the problem but you may need a tow into port at some stage), send an Urgency alert and make a Pan Pan voice call on Channel 16.

- Pan-Pan, Pan-Pan, Pan-Pan
- All Ships, All Ships, All Ships
- This is yacht Fairwind MMSI No 235086183, Call Sign GION6.
- My position is 50°47'.2N by 001°17'.5W.
- I have lost the use of my rudder.
- I am trying to fix it, but I may require a tow into port.
- I am a 30 foot sailing boat and there are two persons on board.
- Over.

Man Overboard

When a man goes in, you need:

- Someone to point at the man overboard (MOB) and keep doing this until he is able to shake him by the hand back on deck
- Someone to throw in the Danbuoy and a lifebuoy
- Someone to hit the MOB button on the chart plotter
- Someone to start the engine
- Someone to throw a throwing line to the MOB
- Someone to hit the DSC Mayday button and to make the voice call
- Someone to ready the retrieval kit
- Someone to head the boat back to the MOB.

That's eight people.

A sailing couple with one in the water leaves one person to do all these jobs.

If you're sailing to windward you can probably spin the boat straight round.

If you are sailing downwind you will have a spinnaker or cruising chute to get rid of before you can turn back to the MOB.

MOB retrieval

Think about how you would get an MOB back on board if he couldn't help himself.

I have spent a lot of time considering this and that is why I came up with MOB Lifesavers that attach to the lifting becket in the life jacket.

When the life jacket inflates the Lifesaver either comes out or is there on top of the bladder available for the rescuer to grab with the boathook and attach the MOB to the boat.

Then you need to consider how you will lift them out of the water and back on deck.

Use a rescue sling to bring them out horizontally and this and the Lifesaver are clipped into a carabiner on the end of a six-part tackle and then haul away.

▲ Live demo in Cowes with Lifesaver retained in pouch on the life jacket and the MOB1 activated.

▶ With a Lifesaver, the MOB has his means of retrieval back on board stowed within his life jacket.

▲ Having got the boat back to or near the MOB, I will throw the throwing line. If he grabs it, you're in business. If not, and he is incapacitated, then you are going to have to get him alongside and get him back on board yourself.

▲ Lifesaver attached to lifting becket and coiled loose in the centre of the jacket so that it floats out on to the water when the jacket inflates.

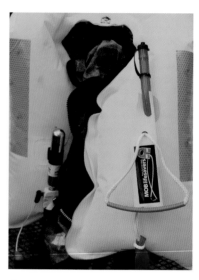

▲ Lifesaver retained in pouch on jacket when it inflates.

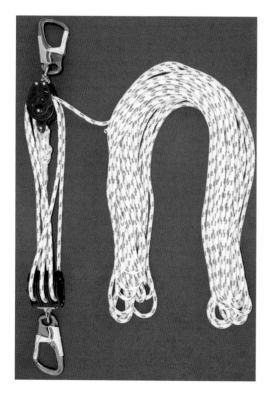

▲ Grabbed with the boathook.

◀ Six-part ratchet block tackle with Kong locking gate carabiners. This is raised on the spinnaker halyard. The tackle has a ratcheted top block, which allows a light person to be able to hold the MOB between finger and thumb.

▲ *MOB Lifesaver in hand.*

▲ *Rescue sling under knees and this and Lifesaver clipped into carabiner.*

▲ *Hauling up the MOB.*

There are other ways of retrieving an incapacitated MOB, using a storm jib, an MOB mat or a Hypo Hoist. And it doesn't matter what you use as long as you have a plan ready in advance. For me, the MOB Lifesaver in the jacket and the six-part tackle are the way to go. Whatever, if you don't have a Lifesaver in the MOB's life jacket and you can't reach down to him and he can't help himself, getting him back on board is not going to be easy, indeed it may not be possible.

Scan the QR code to watch a video of MOB Lifesavers.

Index